Mother's
Song

JOHN SHERRILL

Mother's Song

HODDER AND STOUGHTON
LONDON SYDNEY AUCKLAND TORONTO

306.88

Scripture quotations are from *The Revised Standard Version of the Bible*, copyright 1946, 1952, c1971, 1973 by the Division of Christian Education of the National Council of Churches of Christ in the U.S.A., and are used by permission.

The hymn: "*O Love That Will Not Let Me Go,*" by George Matheson, is copyrighted by Novello & Co., Ltd. and is reproduced by permission of their representative, The Theodore Presser Company, Bryn Mawr, Pennsylvania 19010.

British Library Cataloguing in Publication Data

Sherrill, John
   Mother's song.
   1. Terminal care—Moral and ethical aspects
   I. Title
   174'.24   R726

20027493

ISBN 0 340 32642 5

Hodder and Stoughton Editorial Office: 47 Bedford Square, London WC1B 3DP.

Tib

CONTENTS

I

"I'm going
back
Thursday..."

I

It was early morning in Hong Kong and my wife Tib and I were about to leave our hotel room for a walk through the city. We wanted to see Hong Kong while we could, for we were nearing the end of the assignment that had brought us here. Next Tuesday, just a week from today, we would be flying to isolated East Maui, in the Hawaiian Islands, for the second leg of this work trip; so we had just these few days left in which to savor the orient.

We really couldn't believe that we were here, in this most exotic of the world's great cities. While I dressed, Tib stood at the window of our hotel room, camera in hand, staring down at the sampans, junks, walla wallas, freighters and warships that spelled out in one glance the history of this fortress island.

But what caught Tib's artistic eye was the scene in the distance. Thunder clouds had formed in the west, great blue-black billows that swirled up over the city. The morning sun, still low in the east, fell on the highrises. As will happen once in a while the sun was lighting the building but not the clouds, so that the offices and apartments glowed gold against that background of dark clouds. As Tib snapped the scene we had no way of knowing that over the next 14 days, our lives were going to be like that, golden beauty set off against one of life's dark backdrops.

But our minds that morning were nowhere near such profound sentiments. We were, in fact, thinking about food.

We'd been working for a couple of hours, there in our hotel room, going over notes from the writing assignment into mainland China. We'd had nothing to eat since a Philippine waiter brought early morning tea and now we were hungry. So we were about to go into the laundry-festooned streets of Hong Kong to find one of the vendors who strip batons of sugar cane to enjoy on the sidewalk.

I'm going home on Thursday.

Just like that the thought appeared in my mind.

It was definite and complete and it came out of nowhere. Going home? The day after tomorrow?

It was a whisper, just a whisper, and it made no sense at all. But neither did it go away, this strange idea that was more knowing than thinking.

As I dressed, slowly, I began to argue with this knowledge that sat there. After all, even though Tib was accustomed to traveling alone, neither of us enjoyed that kind of trip. And we still had a week of interviewing work to do here in Hong Kong. Besides, there was no *reason* to go back to the States now. Everything was fine there! There'd been no phone calls from the office, no urgent letters, no telex had been waiting for us when we came out of China. Our three married children and our grand-daughter were all well, so far as we knew.

True, we'd gone through a tense few days trying to decide whether or not to take this trip at all because of my 82-year-old mother's slowly waning strength. But she was comfortable in her cheerful room at Westminster Terrace in Louisville, Ken-tucky. I was almost certain that it couldn't be Mother because we had the people there at the nursing home primed to cable us at any change in her condition.

Tib put her camera down next to the tea tray that still sat on the window seat. "What's the matter, John? You've been standing with one shoe on for two minutes."

So I told her about the thought that had appeared in my mind so unexpectedly.

Then another strange thing happened. Ordinarily, Tib would have helped me examine an experience like that by asking questions. At the very least she would have tried to safeguard one central part of our plans. What about our little honeymoon on Hawaii! There was not another house within sight of Tay and Lowell Thomas' cabin where Tib would be working on a novel with Tay. Before Tay arrived, Tib and I were to have a week alone there, just the two of us. Were we to forego that time together simply because of some nameless impression that I should go home?

But—remarkably—Tib didn't ask those questions. It was as if both of us knew there was a subtle imperative here that had very little mental content.

"Thursday," I repeated, the restlessness continuing to play itself out. "I believe I'm to go home day after tomorrow."

Tib took a sip of cold tea and put the cup down quickly. "That's not much time."

The decision was made just like that.

It wasn't until Thursday morning, riding down the elevator on my way to catch the airport limousine, that Tib said, "Do you know *why* you're going home?"

I shook my head. The certainty was as strong as ever, the reason as mysterious.

I found a seat in the limousine. The motor started. "I'll telephone you," said Tib through the open window, "when I get to Hawaii."

The limousine swung out into the hotel entrance circle and I waved goodbye to Tib, standing more than a little forlornly beneath the canopy.

On the plane I got my favorite seat just behind the bulkhead on the port side of the aircraft. Below us were the scores of islands that dot the sea around Hong Kong. I was staring beyond them across the vastness of mainland China when I remembered a phrase from the Bible. Word of Knowledge. It was one of God's gifts, the occasional imparting of knowledge to us in a manner that is direct, Mind to mind, surpassing the usual means of communication.

I felt a slight racing of my heart. Could it be that this was that sort of experience? Time would tell.

II

"I know why
I had to
come home"

II

The Clipper Lounge at Tokyo Airport was filled with travelers waiting for the continuation of our flight to Los Angeles. Except for a low-voiced conversation here and there, no one was talking much. As if to compensate for the library-like hush, the blonde hostess at the desk spoke too loudly as she tried to reassure a slightly heavy, elderly woman that take-off would be on time. The lady, dressed in a beige wool suit, reminded me of my mother.

A squat Japanese woman in a black smock wanted to clean away rice crackers that someone had spilled on the Pan Am-blue rug. With bows and smiles she asked me to move, so, since it was almost departure time, I used the occasion to go back to the airplane. Boarding ahead of me was the beige lady who looked like Mother. She even walked with a cane, the way Mother did. She turned to the left and hobbled away from me into the First Class section.

I stepped past my sleeping seatmate, buried myself again in my nest of dark-blue pillows and blankets, and turned on my headset. Mendelssohn: about mid-point in what was already the third repeat of "Pan Am Classics in Concert." For some reason I could not get the beige lady out of my mind.

Then I sat up.

Why. . . of course. . . there was not the slightest doubt about it. I was going to Louisville to see my mother.

Strange, because I'd just been there.

I settled back again in my seat. How often I'd made the trip from our home in New York back to my childhood home in Louisville, Kentucky, especially these last four years since Mother entered a nursing home.

Before she fell four years ago, Mother, at 78, had been living by herself in her own house in Anchorage, Kentucky, just outside Louisville. Her home, "Talisman," was brick, L-shaped ranch which she and Dad built for their retirement a quarter of a century earlier. Dad had not lived to enjoy the new house. As she reached her late seventies we often asked Mother if she didn't want someone to stay with her at Talisman. Absolutely not! After all, she still drove her own car, still did her own housework, traveled abroad, lectured, and was planning another book. In short she was not, she pointed out, an old lady.

So she was alone when she fell and broke her hip that warm May day four years ago.

She was not discovered before shock and trauma had been added to the damage of a broken hip. The doctors doubted that Mother would ever return to Talisman. She'd need skilled nursing care for a long time to come.

And skilled care she'd found at Westminster Terrace, a Presbyterian retirement facility which she herself had chosen ". . . for when I get old." At first she'd been upstairs in the total care unit of the Terrace. For the past three years, however, she'd been well enough to live in a pleasant room downstairs at the Terrace, where people were fairly independent.

I smiled as I remembered that room of Mother's, which I'd visited just three weeks ago before coming on this trip to China. How much of herself, her warmth and her color, was in that single room. She'd turned it into a real home with her window plants and her twin decorating themes of butterflies and roses.

As far as I knew, all was well with Mother. What, then, I asked myself on that flight back to the States, was this mysterious urging to go to Louisville. What, for that matter, was a Word of Knowledge! Didn't I remember writing something in the flyleaf of my Bible. . . .

I dug out my travel Bible, unzipped it and sure

enough found a list of the Gifts of the Spirit which I'd noted on the front cover. There they were, dramatic manifestations which we hear about all the time. Healings. Miracles. Faith. Prophecy. And right in the middle of that list from First Corinthians was Word of Knowledge. This gift, according to my notes, was "The impartation of knowledge by the Spirit in a manner by-passing the senses. Often associated with change."

One thing was clear, if this were a Word of Knowledge I did not have to work to receive it. The Word came very naturally, and out of the blue.

It was all so natural, in fact, that I found myself wondering if my imagination had not been working overtime.

The long flight from Tokyo was almost over. A female voice came over the public address system, jolting me from drowsiness in my nest of blue blankets. The stewardess announced in her stamped-metal voice that we'd soon be landing in Los Angeles, so would we please pass our headsets to the aisle. Off went my concert.

Everything seemed out of focus. The suspended sensation that had begun during the flight-break in Tokyo continued to hang over me. Time was out of whack, for one thing. We had passed the international date line and today was yesterday. Place was out of joint, too. The view outside my hotel window, which should have been sampans and walla wallas was instead the parking lot of the Holiday

Inn at Los Angeles airport. Time and place, out of gear. And yet at another level I had never felt so in touch with reality. Some mystic truthfulness was abroad.

I'd promised Tib that I wouldn't even call my secretary until I had gotten some sleep. When I did place the call I was confident I'd learn what crisis had brought on this mysterious urging to come home. Was Mother all right? I asked. Yes; there was no news from Louisville. Perhaps it was the children? No, no message from them. A crisis at the office? No, the office was getting along beautifully. I was more puzzled than ever! Why had I left Hong Kong, where I was clearly needed, to come back here where I was not?

I left my number and went out to lunch.

And now it was later that same day. I had come back to my room overlooking the parking lot to find my call light blinking. I picked up the phone.

"There's a message for 607?"

"Your office has been trying to reach you. Call your secretary as soon as possible."

I got the office on the phone. My sister, Dr. Mary Durham, who lives in Washington, D.C., had left word to get in touch with me, even if I were on the Great Wall.

"What's the matter!" I asked my secretary.

"I'm afraid your mother has pneumonia."

Silence. "Where's Mary now?" I asked at last.

"Half way between Washington and Louisville."

I hung up and looked at the digital clock on the radio. Four in the afternoon; it would be 7:00 P.M. in Washington. I dialed and got my brother-in-law on the line.

"John! They reached you!" said Hugh. "Are you calling from China?"

"I had to come home early." How could I explain *why* I'd come early. "How's Mother?" I asked. "Do you have any more facts?"

But there was nothing to report that I didn't already know. Hugh kept repeating how good it was to have me back in the States right now. I left my hotel phone number with him. Mary reached Louisville too late to call that night but early the next morning the phone rang. Mary, who is usually so calm, was agitated as she reported how glad she was that Mother was at Westminster Terrace.

"The Terrace? I thought she was in the hospital."

"No. They have her on antibiotics at Westminster."

"Can she talk on the phone?"

"No."

"I'll come right away."

"Good," Mary said. "I want so much to stay but. . . wouldn't you know. . . I have a patient in crisis!" Mary is a psychologist. "I *should* be back in Washington Sunday night."

It was a frustrating trip to Louisville. I had long layovers in Denver and Chicago and when I got to Louisville, Mary's plane had already left, taking her back to her patient. I drove through the jonquils and forsythia of Kentucky April out to the Admiral Benbow Motel, then drove on to the Terrace.

As I pushed open the glass doors of Westminster Terrace I found that I was very glad to be here. A face new to me was bent over her paperwork at the nurses' station so I didn't stop but turned right and walked rapidly across the high-sheen vinyl floor toward Mother's room, imagining in pleasant anticipation what her one-room home would be like today. I wondered if the narcissus bulbs, which I'd brought to her just before we left for China, were in bloom now among her cheery butterflies and roses.

The door to Mother's room was closed and—how peculiar!—her name was no longer posted outside. The rectangular, brass name-plate holder was empty.

I knocked. No answer, so I pushed open the door.

The overwhelming smell of clorox met me. I stepped in. Mother's room was stark empty. Her bed, stripped, sat in the eye-smarting disinfectant fumes. Not one of Mother's things was left in her brown room. Every butterfly, every rose gone. Gone was the philodendron, gone the family pictures. I slid open her closet door. Gone were her dresses, gone the suit that she always wore when we took her out to dinner.

I wheeled around, strode to the new nurse at the administration station.

"Where is Mother. . . where is Mrs. Sherrill?" I caught myself and controlled the tone of my voice. "Helen Sherrill?"

"She's been moved," said the nurse, putting down her pen and standing. Odd. Why did she stand? "Upstairs."

Upstairs! Mother had been on Skilled Care on the second floor for months after her fall. She hated it up there.

I whirled around and almost ran to the elevator, pushed the button, remembered how slow the contraption was and took the stairs instead. A little out of breath I stood now in front of the all-too-familiar nurses' station on Skilled Care.

"I'm John Sherrill. Could you tell me which is Mother's room?"

The petite, brown-eyed nurse pointed down the hallway. "Room 245," she said

I walked toward the end of the hall, looking for 245.

Mother's white-uniformed companion, who had been with her since her fall, Cennie McClure, was just coming out the door of the room, her eyes downcast.

"Cennie?" I said. Cennie looked up and managed an enthusiastic welcome-home-from-China! "How are you Cennie?" I asked.

"Oh, I'm fine, John. But your mother's not. I'm so glad you're here."

Cennie turned and stepped back through the door of 245. I followed into the hospital-like whiteness and froze.

There, in the nearer of two hospital beds, was a restlessly tossing figure which I could almost not recognize. Mother's eyes were closed. Her face, powder-pale, worked constantly. Plastic tubes ran downward from bottles that were hanging upside-down on the arms of a boom over her head.

"Hello, Mother."

She did not respond.

I stepped forward hesitantly and froze again as a new realization gripped me. My eyes traveled down the raised, barred sides of the hospital bed and I realized what I was seeing.

Those plastic tubes which ran from the upside-down bottles above Mother's head were connected to two I.V.'s. The needles, hidden beneath adhesive, were imbedded in each of Mother's arms. I stared, unbelieving. For her restless, constantly moving wrists were *tied* to the bars.

All I could do was stare. A groan came from Mother. There was *no* way she could free herself from those gauze fetters that tied her to bars. I looked around, Cennie, a little plump in her white uniform, stood just behind me, stoney, silent.

I turned back toward Mother. The eyes remained closed, but she was never still. Once, when I was in high school, I saw a butterfly that had been pinned to a board while it was still alive. Constantly, constantly, Mother fluttered, tugging, occasionally giving a determined flurry of effort.

I spoke to Cennie. "I'll be back," I said. As I turned to leave I noticed the lady who was Mother's room-mate, a thin figure with big eyes, and then I noticed one more thing before leaving. Someone had brought Mother a single yellow-and-gold Talisman rose. The Talisman was Dad's favorite. The flower sat on the white built-in dresser, all that remained of Mother's identity.

I walked down the hall which was busy with nurses and aides and therapists padding about to the tune of hollow-sounding page calls over the intercom. The hazel-eyed duty nurse looked up. "It's sad to see her so distressed," she said.

It was the kind of caring I'd come to expect here at the Terrace. Even so it was hard to keep the edge out of my voice as I asked why Mother had been tied down. They just didn't have any choice, the nurse said. Mother refused to swallow the oral antibiotics the doctor ordered. They tried giving her antibiotics intravenously but every time they succeeded in finding a vein Mother snatched the needles out.

I went back to 245.

"Cennie?" I said, nodding toward the hallway.

Cennie stepped out and together we walked down to a sunny window garden by the elevator, where Mother and I had so often visited. Twice, on the way to the alcove, staffers stopped me to say they were sorry about Mother. We sat down next to the greenery.

"I guess Mary just couldn't bring herself to tell me over the phone about Mother being tied down," I said.

"She wanted you to get your own reaction."

"What was hers?"

"Mary's? She had a fit," said Cennie.

Cennie filled me in on recent events. For a while, after Tib and I left for China three weeks earlier, Mother had been fine. A minor skin condition which had put her in Suburban Hospital cleared up beautifully. Mother came home to the Terrace. Then, about ten days ago her mind and body began to slip. She became confused. She lay on her bed in her butterfly-and-roses room downstairs on the first floor of the Terrace, coming out of her disorientation only occasionally and then to speak about dying.

"Dying?"

"She was serious," Cennie said. "Remember how she and I used to joke about never being able to diet? Well, starting about ten days ago I couldn't get her to eat *enough*."

Cennie said she'd wheel Mother into the dining area and coax her to try something. "Do you know what she'd do? She'd spread her food around like a kid who doesn't like spinach." Cennie laughed. "I'd catch her in the act!"

I could just imagine the domestic warfare. Cennie vs. Mother! But Mother—as usual—had won. About a week ago, Cennie went on to say, Mother began to have trouble breathing. She lay in her bed downstairs and wheezed and coughed and began to run a fever. Mother's doctors decided that it would accomplish nothing to move her to the hospital. But they did take her out of her room downstairs bringing her up here to Skilled Care.

And they stripped her room!

That, more than all else, said to me that no one

expected Mother to return to the first floor. They'd moved her up here permanently. That move was the message. No one really thought Mother would recover. Yet they were keeping her alive because that was the medically correct thing to do.

"What's in the bottles?" I asked Cennie.

"You'll have to ask the doctor. Glucose solution and antibiotics, I understand."

"She wouldn't take medicine on her own, then?"

Cennie shook her head. "Not even for me. And I know all her tricks." Cennie ironed out her white slacks with her hands.

The elevator doors opened slowly. A young man wheeled out a cart of lunch trays. Cennie and I were silent there in the patch of sun on the second floor of the Terrace. After a while we went back into Room 245. All I could do was stand, helpless, beside the bed with its barred sides. Mother lay with her eyes still closed but a tear track now crossed her cheek. I reached over with my forefinger and wiped it away. The constant arm movement continued, the feeble struggle against those flimsy gauze strips which tied her to the bars of her bed.

"Let me visit with her for a while?"

Cennie nodded and left. I excused myself to Mother's neighbor in the bed next to the window and drew the curtain. I bent down so that my face was close to Mother's.

"It's Johnny, Mother," I said, using my childhood name. "Mary's just left and I'm here now. I don't know whether you can hear me or not, but. . ."

I hoped that the tossing would stop when I spoke,

but it did not. I took Mother's hand in my own, which was difficult because of the gauze knot. Her hand pulled at me. . . or was it pulling at the strip on her wrists? She groaned softly.

"I wish you could hear me," I said. Was that a squeeze? Almost, almost I sensed a tightening of her hand in mine, but who could say! Other than that perhaps-imagined-reply there was no sign. No slowing of the tugs on her restraints, no flicker of her eye, no speeding up or slowing down of her breathing.

A nurse came in. She looked at Mother and shook her head. "I think I'll turn her," she said. She untied Mother's left hand.

Instantly, before the nurse could stop her, Mother's free hand swept across her body to her right arm. With awkward fingers she began to grope and claw and pull at the adhesive which held the needle in her vein.

"Mrs. Sherrill!" The nurse snatched at Mother's left arm. "Here now," she said, "we can't do that."

She forced Mother's hand back to the bars on the near side and struggled to tie the gauze again. I wasn't going to help her.

Finally the nurse stood up, her hair disheveled. "She doesn't like those restraints does she, poor dear."

The nurse left. Mother and I conversed for a while. We did not dialogue, however, for at no point did Mother respond. We "talked" for half an hour, but it was utter frustration. In the end all I could do was hold her hand.

Sitting in silence by Mother's bedside, I allowed something to surface which my conscious mind had been avoiding.

Mother had little fear of death, but she did fear a bad dying. Like most of us, she dreaded the idea of being incapacitated, and then being hooked up to machines, put on chemicals, fed intravenously and kept alive artificially.

Nine years ago, when she was in excellent health, Mother had written out a Living Will which she distributed to a dozen family members. Our copy was in the safe deposit box in our bank in Chappaqua, New York. It was a statement which instructed all concerned that, in the event of irreversible deterioration, we were not to take extraordinary measures to prolong her life.

A band of fear tightened across my forehead. Were we at this very juncture? Had we reached that hitherto unthinkable moment when deterioration could not be reversed and when even so Mother was being kept alive?

As I sat there in Mother's all-white room, holding her hand, I recalled the last time the subject of the Living Will had come up between us, only a few months ago. Tib and I had flown in from New York for a visit with Mother. That day we took her to her favorite Louisville restaurant, the Captain's Quarters, situated right at the edge of the Ohio River. As we struggled out of our car at the restaurant entrance I looked at my watch and noted the time.

We had developed a yardstick for measuring the state of Mother's health: how long did it take us to get to our table by the window at the Captain's Quarters?

And that day we weren't doing too well. Mother's spirits were high, but it was step-wait-step all the way. "Who can use an old body!" Mother sighed as she settled her 82 years heavily into her chair at the window.

We were just beginning to ruin our appetites on the cheese toast-points in the bread basket when Mother said, apropos of nothing,

"Do you still have a copy of my Living Will?"

My first reaction was to duck the question. "Oh come *on*, Mother," I said, laughing. "Any instruction you have for your doctor, just tell him."

"I already have. Do you have a copy of the Will?" she asked again politely but definitely.

"Yes. It is in our safe deposit box."

"What's the date on it?"

"I don't remember. Eight or ten years ago," I said. "I'm sure it's valid."

Privately, I considered the whole matter academic. Of *course* if Mother's mind and body ceased to operate she would not want to be kept alive artificially. Nobody would! But was this decision in our control today? Didn't doctors and courts decide such matters? We had a friend, Etta, 94, who had been kept alive in a state institution for more than ten years. Despite her pleas to be allowed to die, the doctors kept her alive with drugs and forced feedings and recently, with the truly heroic measure of amputating a leg. That day at the Captain's Quarters, as I watched Mother and Tib across the table I found myself thinking:

It's not death, but a prolonged dying that terrifies people.

It's the fear of no longer being in control, of having chemicals and machines determine what happens to you.

Mother picked up another toast-point. "Would you read it to me as soon as you get home? I want to be sure everything is in order."

"Mother, I know it's okay."

"But I want to be sure." She was not going to let the subject lie until she checked it out herself. I recognized that tone of voice from my childhood. It was Mother's heels-planted, tenacious stubbornness at work. Once she'd made up her mind she had a forceful way of hanging on. She'd made up her mind now. "I want you to read it to me when you get home. Would you do that?"

"Of course."

"Good. Now, pass me the menu, would you please?"

Later that same afternoon, after we'd left the Captain's Quarters and had taken Mother back to the Terrace, Tib and I carried coffee up to our motel room at the Admiral Benbow.

"Do you think a Living Will would make a difference?" I asked Tib. "Take Etta. If she had signed such a will wouldn't they have chopped off her leg anyhow?"

Tib took off the plastic lid from her coffee container, tore a small V at the edge of the top, put it back on and sipped. "I think, John Sherrill," she said, "that you're hostile toward the whole medical profession."

I was taken aback by her remark. It had never occurred to me *not* to be at odds with doctors on this issue of dying. Etta was an objective, real look inside the heart of medicine, I felt, and I didn't like what I saw. I read black motives into their steps to keep that poor lady alive; macho, greed, a growing tendency to treat people as "cases." I felt frustrated by the fact that some stranger will be able to say what happens to me when I can no longer defend myself.

I said so.

"I know," said Tib, sipping at the V. "But I don't see it that way. I think technology has outrun us for a bit, that's all. I think the real problem is history."

I had to laugh. That was *just* like Tib. History! But she went on to remind me that after 4,000 years medicine had undergone its first radical revolution within the last half century, especially in the field of growing-old-and-dying. Before then, medicine could only diagnose an old person's ailments and predict the course of deterioration and perhaps alleviate some discomfort. Then along came antibiotics, dialysis, transplants, microsurgery, chemotherapy. Suddenly, doctors could actually affect the span of life. Medical technology outstripped the humane and also the theological questions raised by keeping a worn-out body alive. Only very recently, in the past few years, had doctors begun to ask themselves, "We can keep this body functioning, but *should* we?"

How did Mother's doctor feel about this, Tib and I

asked ourselves.

We were silent for a moment. "Why don't you call him?" said Tib.

I looked at my watch. It was 4:30 in the afternoon. With luck Mother's regular physician, Dr. Thomas Murrow, would still be in the office. I picked up the phone and dialed.

Dr. Murrow was in and yes, he could take the call. After a few politenesses I said, "I have one specific thing I want to bring up. I believe Mother has told you that if she ever becomes incapacitated and can no longer speak for herself, she doesn't want you or the hospital to take heroic measures to keep her alive."

There was a pause. I found myself immediately on the defensive. Here we go, I said to myself. There'll be a thousand complications and ten thousand reasons why we really can't pay attention to that kind of sentiment.

But I was wrong.

"I'm looking at your mother's records, just to be sure," Dr. Murrow was saying. "Yes the chart is marked *No Code 300*."

"No 'Code 300?' What does that mean?"

"Just what she asked for. We are to take no extraordinary measures to keep your mother alive if she becomes unresponsive."

And with that, Dr. Murrow and I finished our conversation. I put down the phone and leaned back in my chair.

"Well, well. . ." I said to Tib. "That was a surprise. There's a revolution going on in medicine. Things are a lot farther along than I thought."

As I summarized my talk with Dr. Murrow I had no way of guessing how soon we'd be looking at this revolution from the inside, as people involved.

There in Mother's room at Westminster Terrace I recalled the rest of our experience with that Living Will. When I got back to Chappaqua I dug out the document as Mother had requested and read it to her over the phone. The short statement was dated February 27, 1972 and it said:

> To Whom It May Concern:
> In the event that my mental condition has deteriorated to the point of mental incapacity, and that in the opinion of a qualified doctor of medicine, there is no probability of return of these mental faculties, I request that my attending physician not initiate but discontinue all supportive and palliative measures for prolonging life.

"The paper is signed and witnessed?" Mother asked.

"Yes."

"And as far as you can tell it's perfectly valid and legal?"

"Yes," I answered. "It's all clear enough."

It was an easy comment to make at the time because the issue was so abstract then.

But now, here in this room with lifesaving fluids slowly, slowly dripping into Mother's system, the full meaning of that document came over me with fearful impact. No one, I knew, could ever fulfill such a will casually or automatically.

I gathered my things and prepared to leave for the day.

"What are your wishes *now*, Mother?" I asked the ceaselessly tossing form.

We knew (from her Living Will), what Mother's wishes were nine years ago; we even knew what they were a month ago, when she insisted we find that will and have it ready. But what about today, right now! At the last minute had life suddenly become unbearably precious; did she want above all else to be kept alive! How would we ever know, since she could no longer speak?

There was so much battling with myself to do. I left Mother's room, walked out to Staff Dining and said goodbye to Cennie until tomorrow. I stepped into the administration office to let them know where I was staying, then headed in the bright afternoon sun toward my car. I knew now the full reason behind that strange nudging to come home from Hong Kong. I was being asked, with my mother and my family, to live through some utterly basic issues that belonged to our time. How did God want us to accept our new ability to keep old bodies alive; did He want us to treat earthly life as such a precious gift from Him that it was always to be protected at all costs and at any age? Or was just the opposite true. . .did the new ability create for the very old a strange miscarriage of the course of life! Was He saying that bodily *death* was precious to Him and needed to be protected since it was His doorway to expand life?

As I let the car warm up, that April afternoon, I sensed that the place to begin my search was in Mother's own life. I'd have to look at her personality. I'd have to live with the eleven months of premature senility that followed her fall. I'd have to look at the fact that we'd allowed antibiotics to be used then. What was the difference between then and now?

And what about ambivalences? After all, relationships are never simple. I certainly had my own ambivalences toward Mother. There were important places where I never had learned to communicate with the lady. Maybe others had the same problem.

I eased my car out of the lot, very aware of the fact that I'd just committed myself to some of the most difficult hours of my life. As I turned away from the Terrace I looked up to the second floor of the red brick building.

"But I won't duck these questions, Mother," I said to the window up there, where Mother lay. "I promise to think about them. Here and now."

III
Mother

III

That April afternoon I drove my rented car all over the limestone hills around Louisville, thinking about Mother.

My mother was a competitor who didn't quite know how to handle that side of her personality. She was the youngest of five children and it was not by accident that Helen Hardwicke earned the nickname Spunky.

I'd like to have known her when she was a girl, growing up in sweltering Sherman, Texas, coping with the tease and put-down of life as the baby of the family. Her father, George Hardwicke, was a manufacturer of cotton gins. The throbbing factory which took up several square blocks of rail siding was a living part of my childhood. We used to visit the factory on hot, summer vacations trips to Sherman. The smell of newly cut leather, the name Hardwicke spelled out in yellow-on-red brick, the petunias planted near the entrance. . .these meant Grandfather Hardwicke to me.

Mother kept forever the spunkiness she gained as a child in Texas. One of the ways this grit showed was in her ability to look for humor in life, as for example when Dad's parishoners found the bourbon bottle under his bed. Mother met Lewis Sherrill while he was in seminary, fell in love, waited while he served in France in the First World War. When Mother and Dad married, their first little church was in Covington, Tennessee, and it was there that Dad got the poison ivy.

Dad hadn't been in his new church a month before he came down with such a bad case of ivy poisoning that it put him to bed. "You know the Tennessee remedy for poison ivy?" a parishoner asked. "Bourbon whisky." The man pulled out a pint, helped Dad smear the liquid all over his welts. Unfortunately the parishoner left Dad's sickroom just before a group of ladies arrived with home remedies of their own. Mother watched as the ladies began to sniff and their frowns began to deepen. But instead of being nonplussed, Mother started to laugh. "Ladies," she said, "this *will* be a story to tell my grandchildren! Lewis doesn't drink, but who's going to believe our poison ivy story?

After all, you've just walked into the manse that is reeking with whisky and you see the new preacher with a bottle of bourbon under the bed!" The story spread through Covington, all right, but not as a scandal.

Mother was an interesting mixture of grace and stubbornness. She was a planner. She mapped out her life down to the details; not all her plans worked out. She wanted a large family, for instance, and ended up with just two children, Mary and me. "Dad got his Ph.D instead," Mother told Mary once. "It was a real choice back in Depression days."

Mother also had to yield to Dad about Talisman. I never realized as a boy that Talisman wasn't Mother's idea of fun. She could never understand the logic of spending all that money on a piece of land and a derelict old building.

Mother and Dad had moved to Louisville, Kentucky, after five years in the pastorate in Covington. Dad became Dean of the Presbyterian Seminary there in Louisville at the end of the 20's when Wall Street was making everybody rich. I remember seeing him set out for the seminary each morning, briefcase in hand and wearing his scratchy gray tweed suit. Then came the crash and the Depression.

"I've got a salary right now, Helen," Dad told Mother one day. "But I may not have one for long. We ought to buy a little piece of land. If the seminary closes we could always live off vegetables and chickens."

The little piece of land he had in mind was a rolling knoll on the edge of Anchorage, Kentucky (a retired sea captain gave the village this name), some miles outside of Louisville.

"That could be our land, Helen," Dad said, driving Mother, Mary (age 10) and me (12) in our Chevrolet out to the country to take a look.

Mother said nothing.

Dad rambled on about the importance of owning land. He quoted Will Rogers, "Buy land, they ain't making it any more."

"How many acres would you have to take care of?" Mother finally asked.

"Just what you see there!" Dad swept his arm over the grassy knoll with one lonesome and unbelievably large maple tree in the middle. "Twenty acres more or less. And a house."

"A *house*?" Mother said, her shoulders sinking. Mother never did enjoy housework. "I don't see any buildings."

So Dad drove us through a catalpa grove on the corner of the land to what at one time had been a home. The house, an old red brick two-floored building, had stood empty for years, an invitation to vandals who broke in looking for treasure that, everyone knew, was buried in the walls. Not a single pane of glass was left intact, not a fireplace mantle without its carved grafitti. But it wasn't the house that interested Dad anyway. It was that land. As he walked over it, wondering if he could stretch his savings to the limit and buy this property, his eyes shone and Mother listened to his plans for raising chickens.

"I think I'll call the place, 'Talisman,' " Dad said.

46

Talisman was the name of his favorite yellow-and-gold rose, one of the varieties he grew in the vacant lot next to our seminary-owned house in Louisville.

With the naming of Talisman Mother knew she didn't have a chance. So, in spite of her secret, negative feelings we bought the land. As far as I know the only chickens ever to grace the property came ready-dressed from the A&P.

But generally Mother's plans *did* work out. When she was in her mid-forties Mother went back to school. Mary and I were in college now, and Mother defied Louisville mores of the day by deciding that she was going to have a career of her own. "I'll get my M.A. in social work then find a job," she announced.

That's what happened, too. As I drove all over Louisville that sunny April afternoon, sorting out my emotions at finding Mother tied to her bed, my route took me past the red brick buildings of the University of Louisville. How proud Dad was when Mother won her Master's and proceeded to get a job at the Child Guidance Clinic, just as her adventuresome spirit had planned. Mother liked to encourage the pioneer in other people, too. She and my wife Tib were close, one independent soul recognizing another. At one point, Mother learned that Tib was having trouble. In the conformist 50s great value was given to being the type of housewife pictured in magazine ads. When Tib decided to spend her mornings writing, and stopped going to the coffeeklatches in our housing development just outside New York City, she opened herself up for criticism and shunning from other mothers in our neighborhood.

"Don't let it bother you, Tib!" Mother argued. "You'll always meet people who want you to conform to their style. If you let them do it, they'll keep you from becoming the person *you're* intended to be."

Some parts of Mother's personality made me angry. She had a compulsive need to control.

That same afternoon, as I drove through Louisville trying to answer basic questions about Mother, I found myself on the River Road and stopped at the Captain's Quarters, where Tib and Mother and I dined so often. I sat at Mother's favorite table looking out at the houseboats and barges working the river and remembered how insistent she had been that day when she asked about her Living Will. At the memory of that minor little scene, a knot formed in my stomach, partly because of her request, but also because of the way her tone made me feel that I had no real choices of my own. I recognized that stomach-knot from boyhood. It came whenever I felt Mother trying to control me.

She didn't attempt to maneuver Dad but she did try with Mary and me. It was always a trauma taking Mother to an airport because she had to be there two hours ahead of time, no matter what our own plans might be. Tib once took a train trip with

Mother. "But I wouldn't do it again,"Tib reported, laughing. "She had a schedule in her lap. I think she asked the conductor six times why the train was running late."

Mother tried to impose her controls on me even when I was an adult. I remember more than one scene that centered around Sunday dinner. Mother and Dad had moved to New York for Dad's final seven years of teaching and they were living in an apartment at Union Theological Seminary. We were often invited there, with our toddler Scott, (and later with our two other children) for Sunday dinner. But many of those lovely occasions were edged with tension. Tib and I were new at the art of getting a play pen and a stroller and a snow suit and a dry child into the car and onto the road and we were sometimes late. True, this was awkward for the cook, but Mother's reaction was extreme. *We* might be late, but dinner wasn't. If the meal was planned for 1:00 it was served at 1:00 whether we were there or not.

I could see all this as just a part of the tapestry of personality. Except for one thing. It kept Mother and me from being able to talk together about faith.

On religious matters there had always been an odd tradition of reticence in our family. Dad held vespers every evening in the living room of our house in Louisville, where we lived most of the year when we weren't at Talisman, but the Bible was expected to speak for itself. One evening when I was a boy I asked Dad if he believed Jesus was God. "What does the Bible say?" he countered.

49

Mother was even more reluctant to speak about her personal convictions. This was cultural, in part; the people she associated with, though committed Christians, were not verbal about their faith. But there was a deeper reason, I think. All her life Mother was wary of hypocrisy, both in herself and in others. The Christians she knew who *did* have much to say about their own commitment often seemed to her the least impressive examples in their daily lives. Mother recognized her own weaknesses— no one saw them more clearly. She made up her mind, I believe, that she was not going to gloss over her short-comings with pious sounding phrases.

At any rate—at least with me—Mother would not talk about her life with God. This silence was a deep disappointment for me. When I was in my 30s I contracted cancer, with the prognosis of an early death. To my surprise, when in my fear I mumbled that I was willing to take the plunge into belief, God took me up on the stumbling confession. Life changed. I survived cancer, and—also to my surprise—my new belief survived as well. The altered outlook began to affect decisions about work and lifestyle.

But I couldn't talk with my parents about this phenomenon of personal faith. Dad died just before he and mother were to leave New York and move into the dream house they'd built on Talisman with money they received by selling off most of the land. Mother stayed on in New York as Dean of Women at the seminary. I tried to talk with her, during those days, about my conversion but she would consistently change the subject. I remember one day when we were having lunch together in a New York restaurant, just the two of us, and I tried to launch into a description of what had been happening to me. Mother must have sensed where I was headed. She called the waitress and asked for a new napkin. Then she asked for another glass of water, then she began to move the silverware about.

"I think I'll have a club sandwich," I said.

Mother squared her silverware away and smiled. "Good. Now do tell me all about the children. . . ."

So I was faced with a dilemma. I respected Mother's shyness and at the same time I felt that she wasn't letting me be myself. Odd, since individuality was a quality she championed with such passion.

I thought, at one point, that she was at last inviting me to open the subject. One bright spring morning, after she too had retired, I was visiting her in her dream house on Talisman.

"Have you seen the new furniture on my Thinking Porch?" Mother asked.

Mother's Thinking Porch was a closet-sized, screened-in nook off one of the bedrooms where she kept her Bible and a private notebook. I thought, when she asked me out to see her quiet place, that perhaps she was leading into that long-hoped-for talk about spiritual life.

I was wrong.

Mother opened the door to her domain proudly, showed me the comfortable all-weather chair she'd bought and chatted about which plants like which kind of light. I paid no attention to the caution signals inside me and moved ahead.

"I just finished reading the Bible cover-to-cover," I said. I picked up Mother's Bible. "Dad would have been proud of me."

"Why?"

"For reading the Bible. I once asked him if Jesus was God and he said to read the Bible."

Mother stared at me with her incredibly blue eyes. She made absolutely no move to break the tension that suddenly hung between us. I felt she was sorry she'd asked me to see the new furniture.

Then Mother said a strange thing.

She stood on that tiny porch amid her flowers and her ceramic butterflies like a person standing in a breached wall.

"People are always trying to maneuver me," Mother said.

Her eyes did not waver. "What do you mean?" I asked.

Mother didn't answer. She just stood there. She, whom I had pigeonholed as a controlling person, was herself terrified of being controlled. It added up. It fitted her youngest-child place in her own family. I tried to soften the edge in my voice. "Do you think *I'm* trying to maneuver you?"

Mother said, "There's a woman at church I can't stand to be around. She is always wanting me to say things a certain way."

"Like what?"

Mother wouldn't answer. We stood toe to toe. The silence stretched on. I broke it at last. "I don't know what to say. This is a part of my life that I want to talk to you about and you're turning me off. I'm not some lady in your church. I'm John."

For the first time since we came out onto her porch the frown lines on Mother's forehead softened. "Of course you're John," she said. Then she turned toward the door. "But so am I Helen. I must move at my pace. Come on, let's have breakfast."

I realized when I reached the kitchen that I still had Mother's Bible in my hand. I put it on the kitchen counter while she fixed eggs and country ham.

We ate in the kitchen, trying to pretend nothing had happened. After we'd pushed aside our plates Mother got up and went to the counter and came back with her Bible.

She handed it to me.

"Read me a psalm, would you?" Mother said off-handedly. Again our eyes held. "It's my favorite book in the Bible," Mother said. "I'd like you to read for me."

It was as close an apology as this proud person could achieve.

IV
Comeback

IV

Right up until the eve of her 78th birthday—five years before the decision I now faced—Mother still lived by herself. On her own, she had selected the apartment she would move to one day, in nearby Westminster Terrace, a Presbyterian retirement complex with health care facility attached.

Mother wanted Tib and me to see the Terrace. On our next visit to Kentucky to celebrate her 78th birthday we piled into her silver-grey Chevy and drove over. The Terrace was a handsome four-story building of one-and-two bedroom apartments where retired people lived in complete independence.

"While we're here we might as well see the nursing care side," Mother said.

She headed down the high-sheen corridor that connected the residential apartments to a lower, two-story, red brick building where people went when they needed medical attention. The first floor of this wing, Mother explained as she showed us around, was for people who needed only light nursing. The second floor which she showed us, too, was like a hospital specializing in care for very old, frail and senile people. Mother hurried Tib and me away from Second as a place that surely had no relevance to *her* plans.

When we got back to Talisman, after that introductory visit to the Terrace, a very ordinary event took place which was to play a role over the next four years of far-from-ordinary events. Mother served tea in her living room by the picture window. We gave her a birthday present, a leaded-glass butterfly to hang in her window.

"I meant to give you something else," said Tib. "But it isn't ready. It's a surprise."

"Tell me," said Mother, her blue eyes alive. "I can't stand surprises."

Tib was standing by the tea cart. She looked at me over her cup.

"Should I?"

I nodded.

"Well," Tib said, and suddenly she blushed. "I've started making you a tote bag, Mother. It's needlepoint and it's taking forever. Only thing I've ever made with my own hands."

Mother got up (a bit heavily) and went over to Tib and put both arms around her. "You're really *making* something for me? With your hands!"

"For your 79th birthday," said Tib. "I promise."

The two didn't say another word, but they held their embrace for a very long time.

Mother's fall came just before that 79th birthday. We did not piece together all the details for some time, but fragment-here, fragment-there the picture became clear. On Memorial Day Mother slipped on a scatter rug in her bedroom and broke her hip. She lay for nobody-knows-how-long, unable to reach the telephone on her night table. She heard a power mower start up nearby and tried to call over it, but the mower just kept on running. At last she heard a car crunch up the drive, a car door slam. Someone was coming toward the house.

"Hello! Thank God! Hello!"

The front doorbell rang. "Yes! I'm in here! I'm in the bedroom!"

The doorbell rang again. Mother shouted desperately now. She whistled her shrill, penetrating whistle, the one that used to bring Mary and me running home for lunch. But the mower drowned her out. The caller rang once more and. . .left.

Panicky now, Mother tried again to reach the telephone. Maybe she could *roll* to it. She put out her left hand, braced it against the floor and pushed herself over until finally she could just reach the telephone cord. Mother gripped the cord and yanked. The instrument tumbled off the night table. Mother couldn't move away. The telephone landed full weight on her head.

Mother came to.

She did not know how long she had been knocked out, but at least the phone lay nearby, the receiver off its cradle and whining. Slowly Mother put her forefinger forward and dialed.

Mary and Hugh arranged to take their vacations right then, to be near Mother while she was in the hospital. I would come down following their stay, so that either Mary or I would be with Mother this first little while after the pin-inserting operation on her hip. The doctor, Mary said on the phone from Kentucky, was not at all hopeful that Mother could return to Talisman. She was going to need skilled nursing care. I telephoned Mother at the hospital. Our conversation went smoothly enough at first, except that I noticed a slurring in Mother's speech. Then she said something that threw me.

"Johnny," she said, using my childhood name, "we really do have to consider the Egyptians."

I let that one sink in.

"What do you mean, Mother?"

"The Egyptians. There'll be trouble if we don't consider the Egyptians."

When I reported this on the phone to Mary, she said she'd noticed similar small nonsensical lapses but nothing severe. The next day, though, Mother's mental condition was worse: she seemed disoriented both as to time and place. Dr. Murrow couldn't say for sure, but all the signs pointed to cerebral arteriosclerosis.

Cerebral arteriosclerosis. The hardening of the arteries of the brain. If that were true, it would be progressive. Mother would soon not be able to distinguish reality from fantasy, or yesterday from today. . . .

On her release from the hospital Hugh managed to get Mother admitted directly to the nursing wing of Westminster Terrace. Mary phoned from Anchorage a week later to report that Mother was settled now in her room on the second floor of the Terrace.

"I'll come down for her birthday," I said. June 24 was just a few days off. Through my mind flashed the memory of our tea party in Mother's living room a year earlier, when Tib promised she'd have the tote bag ready for her 79th birthday. Well, the handmade bag was in front of me now, sitting on the mantle in our living room, evidence that sheer stick-to-itiveness can achieve wonders.

"I'll bring the tote bag," I said to Mary—everyone knew about that bag!

And so it was, a few days later, that I was parking my rented car at the Terrace. I stepped out carrying a tote-bag-sized package. My earlier impression of the Terrace was confirmed. I felt the warmth of the place in the landscaping, in the blossoming flower-and-vegetable gardens, in the patios-with-umbrellas. How ironic, though, that I should be going to see

Mother on the second floor of the nursing unit, the one part of the institution which she didn't like. Mother resisted Second not because of the care, which was "absolutely tops," she had reported to us when she was making her original, characteristically thorough investigation of the Terrace. The care was excellent, but many of the patients were senile. Mother equated the second floor with the loss of minds and rejected absolutely the thought that some day she might not be in charge of her own.

Yet now here I was, going to see her on that same floor. I stepped out into the sunlit hall of Second. An alcove with houseplants in a window was to my right; the central nurses' station was to my left.

"I'm John Sherrill," I said to the duty nurse. "Helen Sherrill's son. Is Mother up and about?"

The nurse put down her paperwork and came around the desk to take my hand. Well, well! It was good to see me. She'd met my sister and her husband; their name was Durham, wasn't it? "Yes." From Washington, D.C.? "Yes." And wasn't my sister a psychologist just like Mrs. Sherrill? "Yes, it runs in the family." Well, well! The nurse led me off to the east end of the floor.

We paused just outside a hospital-wide door.

"You need to be, well, prepared, for your mother's condition, Mr. Sherrill."

"How do you mean?"

"Her hip is healing just beautifully. Her mind, though. . . ."

She opened the door and I froze, a wave of pressure hitting my eyes. Mother sat in a wheelchair, facing the window. She was slumped over a little sideways. Her hand kept moving restlessly to her gray hair, combing it with her fingers.

"Shall I go in with you?" said the nurse.

"No, thank you. It's okay."

The nurse, well, she was right there if I needed her. She turned on her white space shoes and walked away.

The second floor room where Mother sat, on that very first of my visits to see her at the Terrace, was white. White spreads on the two beds, (the other one was empty), white curtains on overhead tracks, white fixtures. It made the room bright, but to me it said that the people here had left their personalities outside.

Mother turned around. Her face was thinner than I'd ever seen it.

"How do you do," Mother said.

I walked closer and pulled up a chair next to her.

Mother looked at me steadily. "I expect you're here to take some more tests? All right. . . ."

"Mother, it's John."

There was no embarrassment, just a shifting of gears. "Johnny!" she said. "How good to see you. I want to move downstairs, John, and they won't let me."

"Happy Birthday, Mother."

"Oh, yes. That's nice of you to remember. How many is it?"

"Seventy nine."

"Think of that!" Her hands stroked the gray hair.

"Tib sent you something. She wishes she could be here."

Mother's eyes shone with delight. She took the package and with awkward fingers tore at the wrapping. "Look!" she said. "How very lovely! And she made it herself!"

"Every stitch." Odd. Mother had confused me with a doctor, but she remembered that Tib had promised a handmade gift. Mother pushed the wheels of her chair. She hadn't got the art yet and the chair refused to go in a straight line, but she eventually managed to steer herself to the window-sill, where sat a few personal belongings, a comb, a package of kleenex, a coin purse. Mother put these into her new tote bag.

"Let's take a walk," Mother said. "We can go out to the elevator where there are green things to look at."

"I'd like that."

I wheeled her chair to the sun-washed garden by the elevator. She continued addressing me as her son. But it slowly crept into my awareness that although Mother was now recognizing me, she was not sitting with me by the elevator on the second floor of Westminster Terrace in Louisville. Instead she was drifting in and out of places and times in the past. At one moment she seemed to be in her office at the Child Guidance Clinic in Louisville. Then she was waiting for an elevator at Barnard College in New York where she had taught. Or she was introducing me to her secretary (in actuality, a young visitor who just stepped off the elevator) at Union

Theological Seminary.

The entire day was an exercise in swinging back and forth in time. Mother, when she was in the now, wanted me to take her down to the first floor.

"I'll be moving down soon, you know," she said as I pushed the elevator button. "Downstairs is where real people live."

I was puzzled by that comment. It couldn't be snobbishness. Mother used to take her vacations riding Trailway buses just to be with all different kinds of people. "Real people" I decided meant people who were in their right minds. Mother wanted to be around people who were alert.

I wheeled her chair out of the elevator and Mother introduced me accurately to the head nurse. She had me make the circuit of the first floor, where she so desperately wanted to move. We looked into the rooms where she would be living, she assured me, "tomorrow." I was surprised, while she was expressing goals, that she did not also speak of moving to the residential apartments in the building next door; but there was a strange realism that ran side by side with her confusion. Mother couldn't quite fantasize living in her own apartment; for now she had First Floor in her sights.

Later that same day, after I had wheeled Mother back to her room on Second I was seated in the office of Dr. Thomas Murrow, Mother's physician. I dreaded asking for the prognosis, and I sensed that Dr. Murrow hated giving it. He took his time spelling out the new, sophisticated scans and computer diagnostics that are available today. The report from the teams cooperating on the tests was this: Mother did indeed have cerebral arteriosclerosis. The condition probably had not come on all of a sudden. In fact, Dr. Murrow said, it could be that this hardening of the arteries in the brain had *caused* the fall.

"And what's going to happen now?" I asked.

"I can only tell you what experience says." He took a breath. "Experience says that your mother's condition is progressive and that it is irreversible."

Six months after her fall all indications were that Dr. Murrow's reluctant prognosis was correct. The bad days came more and more frequently. Mother's lawyer recommended that Mary and I sell Talisman. The house was suffering from half a year of neglect and now winter was coming on. Mary got to Louisville ahead of me and met my plane. It was easy to spot Mary when she came to meet a plane. She was petite and always tried to stand in the very front of the crowd of visitors, a gray-haired, relaxed lady dressed usually in a tailored suit and Old Maine Trotters. Sure enough she was there in front of the crowd now, and wore a blue suit.

Mary seemed intense an hour later though as we stood on what had once been a lawn at Talisman. We could see for ourselves the damage that was being done by neglect. Weeds were coming up in the driveway, branches were down, there was a broken window. Inside the house it was clammy. I couldn't get the furnace working. Details spoke of sudden change. Shriveled flowers fell out of a vase. In the refrigerator a half-eaten can of tuna wore a thick coating of mold. Mother had fallen on Memorial Day weekend. The Louisville *Courier Journal* on the kitchen table predicted a heavy traffic-death toll. In Mother's bedroom the scatter rug that had caused all the trouble was still askew on the floor.

Somehow we got through those days of closing the house and putting it up for sale.

The hardest part was not being sure Mother understood us when we told her what we were doing.

As the months passed, it seemed impossible that mother would be able to move down to First. Her dominant fantasy was that she was taking a train trip. Any scraping chair, any diesel horn from a distant freight, would be enough to trigger it. She would mix reality and unreality. "Hello, Donnie," she might say, when our second son was visiting. "I'm really glad you came to see me, but it will have to be a short visit. The train is about to leave as you can see."

Our instructions from the staff, at such times, were gently and repeatedly to draw Mother back to the here and now: "I'm glad to be here, too, Grandmother," Donn would answer. "But we're not in a train station. We're in Westminster Terrace."

Sometimes the reminder succeeded. Increasingly,

it did not. But never did she relinquish her plan for moving down to First. Throughout these months of distress the Spunky side of her personality became very evident. So many of the patients on Second had drifted into a kind of passive acceptance. Not my mother! As her leg healed, she graduated from wheelchair to walker. Whenever I came to see her, the first business of the day was a long, limping walk through First.

Having a goal, even a confused one, stood her in good stead as January came, then February and March with the inevitable outbreak of flu among Westminster's elderly. With the aid of antibiotics Mother battled back from each infection. "The arteriosclerosis may have affected her mind," one nurse told me admiringly, "but it certainly hasn't touched her spirit. I never met anyone with a stronger will to get well."

Mother's determined will, in fact, was soon creating problems for herself and those around her. She was no sooner out of bed and getting about again with the walker than she took to making solo trips downstairs—to the distress of first-floor residents and staff.

The problem was not so acute during the day, when there was generally someone upstairs to intercept her. But at night, with a smaller staff, Mother's wandering created tension all around.

Mary telephoned after a visit. "They keep finding her in the elevator at two or three in the morning."

"How are they handling it?"

"I'll tell you how." Mary's voice was indignant.

"The only way they can—with sedation."

I felt a wave of anger sweep over me. The anger wasn't directed at the Terrace, but at life itself.

"There could be another answer for Mother," Mary said. "She could hire a companion. It would be expensive, but then if Mother wanted to walk, she could walk. Whenever she pleased. It'd be good for her."

The decision was an easy one to make. Mother and Dad had husbanded their resources for many years for one reason—independence as they grew older. Well, being able to walk about was the most primal kind of independence there was. Mary and I had powers of attorney, and we decided without much discussion to use Mother's money in this way.

Many fine women came to keep Mother company over the following months, but one was to play a special role. Her name was Cennie McClure. Cennie was a little on the plump side, short-haired, always dressed in the same uniform—white dacron trousers, white over-blouse. Cennie used to brag about her upbringing.

"My daddy just had one arm," she said. "But with that one arm he had enough love to hug six children."

It was the policy at the Terrace for employees to call residents Mr. or Mrs. So-and-so, rather than use first names. We appreciated that; it accorded with the dignity of these senior people. But Cennie McClure was different. Within a week, at Mother's insistence, it was Cennie and Helen. When the administration reminded Mother of their last-name policy Mother returned to the present long enough to take a stand. Cennie was not employed by the Terrace; if she, Helen Sherrill, chose to be on a first name basis with someone she had hired, then that was no one's business but her own.

"Your mother," the nurse who told me this story summed up, "is a scrapper."

Then, eleven months after her fall, on one of our routine calls to the Terrace, Cennie was excited:

"I don't want to be too hopeful, you know?" she said. "I mean, we've had good days before. But Helen's had several in a row now. She's so cheerful and bright."

I flew down immediately; Mary would follow as soon as she could get away from her practice. The next morning I called Tib from Mother's room, upstairs at the Terrace.

"Honey," I said, "Mother wants to speak to you. . . ."

Cennie and I helped Mother over to the phone. She sat on the edge of her white bed in her white room on the second floor. "Tibby! What do you make of this old lady coming back after eleven months away?" Her voice was bright, unslurred. Mother replied in answer to a question from Tib that she could remember the fall in detail but almost nothing in the weeks and months that had followed.

That morning Mother picked up Tib's brown-and-orange tote bag, and she and Cennie and I went for a shuffling, slow walk down the hall of Second.

There was a mood of celebration on the floor. Mother stopped to say hello to staff and patients. The feel was exactly that of someone coming back from a long trip where she recognized faces but couldn't remember names.

Of course Mother wanted to visit First. She went straight to the administration office where she inquired about moving down. The superintendent, as baffled as the rest of us by the day-and-night change in her, tried to be non-commital. Mother was having none of it.

"You think I could slip back again. Well, I suppose I might. But in the meanwhile, I would like my application considered as of today, please."

Dr. Murrow was mystified, too. "You ask what's happened? Frankly, I don't know. Medicine doesn't know. What caused the loss of faculties in the first place or what caused the return—both are mysteries."

Was it prayer? We had started off eleven months ago praying heroically, trying to believe in a complete healing. Sunday after Sunday we included Mother's name in the prayers-for-the-sick at church. Wednesday evenings we kept our prayer group alert to each new development. I prayed for her in person, rather shyly, with the ancient rite of the laying-on-of-hands.

But as the months passed, to be honest, we had begun to believe the computer print out of her brain wave pattern. We trusted the diagnosis, not the Bible's promises of healing. More and more our prayers stopped with asking to relieve her anxiety, to calm her agitation.

I wondered often about this after her comeback. On only one thing were all the doctors agreed: cerebral arteriosclerosis could not have been the correct diagnosis. Cerebral arteriosclerosis, as everyone knows, is irreversible.*

Mother's sometime abrasive, always fiery insistence that she get off Second finally paid off. She rejected the atmosphere of senility which for her, she said, was as contagious as the flu. She telephoned us in New York on the day they found a single room for her down on First.

"I won, John," she reported with excitement. "You'll like my new home. Cennie and I are decorating it in purples and lavenders and greens. No more whites!"

We urged Cennie to stay on and she did. She arrived daily in her camel-colored '78 Nova to take Mother to the stores, to the dentist, to an expanding list of social engagements. On my next visit, after showing me proudly around the new home she'd created on the first floor, Mother asked me to drive her out to Talisman. "Just for a last look."

The house, under its new owner, was freshly painted, sitting well back from the road on its deep

---

* For an account of the helpful role Scripture played for us during this time of senility and amnesia, see *My Friend the Bible*, Chosen Books, Lincoln, VA 22078

lawn. It was mid-day but no cars were in evidence. So Mother and I nosed into the long driveway, our tires crunching on the gravel. If Mother was remembering the pain-filled hours a year ago, lying on the floor in her bedroom hearing people come and go, trying to make her screams heard above the noise of a mower—if she was thinking of these things, she said nothing.

I stopped the car and turned off the motor. Neither Mother nor I spoke as thoughts crowded around us. As we sat there in the driveway I appreciated something about Mother. She might be a lady who planned her life more carefully than most of us dare to do. But she also understood seasonality.

I looked at her now. She had gotten a little heavier over the past year of enforced inactivity, although she wore a well-tailored beige suite that hid the bulges more or less successfully. She sat there looking at the spring glory which she herself had planted over the years.

"I guess we should go," Mother said at last.

I reached over and turned the ignition key, but I didn't immediately start down the drive. My eyes traveled to Mother's Thinking Porch.

"It must be very hard, leaving," I said.

"Oddly, it isn't," Mother answered. "There's a right time for everything—this is a time to say goodbye." She opened her hands as if to say, "It's over," and with that gesture she let Talisman go.

Mother's appreciation of the seasons of life became more and more important to her:

Two years went by. How I used to enjoy going into that room of hers on the first floor of the Terrace. Amazing, how Mother had managed to turn that institutional room, with its tell-tale curtain track in the ceiling, into a home. She moved around the material she had to work with, a few pieces of good furniture, books, pillows and blankets, so that the room was perpetually different and new, like the inside of a kaleidoscope.

Family pictures went on walls and dressers: photos of Mother's parents, from Sherman; a second grouping of Dad's family; pictures of Mary and me as children; pictures of her grandchildren and great-grandchildren. In the window she hung her collection of glass butterflies—those frolicking, light-as-air creatures that were her special symbol. She had butterflies on her scarves and pins, on throw pillows and the guest towels she hung in her tiny bathroom. To me they represented Mother's independent, don't-pin-me-down spirit—just as the roses she always had around her stood, I believe, for Dad.

Oh yes, there was also the symbolically-important refrigerator.

I don't know how Mother managed to talk the Terrace into letting her have that frig. It certainly didn't help her waistline. She and her Cennie were forever fighting the bulge battle and that little unit was their Trojan horse. In it Mother kept good cheese and whole wheat bread. . . and candy. . . and ice cream. But it let Mother, crucially for her own self-worth, be hostess to the sizable circle of residents, friends and family who dropped in for tea or an afternoon of bridge.

This, I began to perceive, was how Mother was using the time that had been given back to her: building, mending, completing relationships. Her life had a kind of purposefulness to it as if she were under obligation to deal with unfinished business. She was, I think, working on parts of her personality that had been abrasive such as, for example, her attitude toward time. Once when Tib and I were late for an afternoon tea, we found that Mother had laid out the makings but had not put on the electric tea kettle. She said nothing about our being late, only that she was really glad to see us. Never in the past would she have had this reaction.

"Now fill me in on Liz," she said. "Is my granddaughter really following in my steps? She's started a Masters in Social Work?"

I was getting close now, I felt, to understanding how Mother felt today about her death. Mending relationships had been part of a *much* larger picture. She had begun to plan again, and this time she was planning. . . her death.

At first this seemed extraordinary to me, but then I realized that all of us think about our deaths; most of us know exactly what we'd want the end to be like. Mother was just a little more explicit about it.

One day Mother let me glimpse this new focus in

her thinking. We'd come back from a long drive, just the two of us, wandering through the old part of Louisville where Germans had settled; and now Mother was getting out cheddar and biscuits from her refrigerator.

"Do you know what happened last week, on one single day?" she said. "Three of my friends here died. Three, John."

Mother hobbled across her room and put the cheese on a card table. She steadied herself against a chair. "I'm the only one left in my family now," she said, not looking at me, seemingly casual. "And I won't be around long."

I started to say something like come on Mother, you'll outlive us all, but changed my mind. "Your family's long-lived, isn't it?" I said, instead.

"Not especially. Most of us have died in our seventies and early eighties." Mother was 81. Her answer came so quickly, without her having to stop to consider, that it was clear to me she'd already asked herself the same question.

Slowly, in that fourth year after her fall, Mother began to speak even more directly about death. From seemingly casual comments I learned that it was a positive thought, like graduating to First, where people were alert, and alive. Once, for example—only once, but what a universe opened when she said it—did she slip into a conversation the fact that she knew she'd see Dad again.

"I count on it, John," she said. "I'll be with him soon."

I guessed that there were other things she

wanted to say but just could not. I suspected that she was doing some building-and-repair on her relationship with God just as she had been doing with family. But—to me at least—she still never spoke about this area of her life. I did buy Mother a large-print edition of the Bible. She thanked me and asked me to read to her. Perhaps it was my imagination but it did seem to me that Mother was asking me to read the Bible to her more frequently, of late. What did that mean, I wondered?

All of us worried as we watched Mother slow down. She slept a great deal. It took a record amount of time to get into the car, or across a restaurant floor. Minor ailments wouldn't go away. One, a skin condition on her forehead, put her in the hospital for a few days, and it was while I was there visiting her that Tib phoned to say we'd received a once-in-a-lifetime invitation.

We'd been asked to go to China on an assignment. All expenses paid! We'd have to leave at once. The idea sounded great but I didn't see how I could go. Mother's condition didn't warrant it.

"At least ask the doctor what he thinks," Tib urged. So I went to see Dr. Murrow and told him about the trip and my hesitancy because of Mother.

Dr. Murrow reassured me. "We don't have a crisis," he said. "Your mother has a very strong constitution; I've rarely seen a stronger one. If it were my mother, I would go."

So we made the decision to go. The timing was perfect because of Tib's longstanding appointment for a work session in Hawaii with Tay Thomas. We rushed to purchase traveler's checks, and books on the orient to read on the plane.

On March 2, we flew to Hong Kong.

Three weeks later, standing at the picture window of our hotel room I suddenly knew: *I'm going home on Thursday*.

And now, here I was leaving the Captains Quarters to head back to my motel. I had driven completely around Louisville since I left Mother a few hours earlier, searching in this nostalgic trip for a clear picture of what she herself wanted.

I knew the answer, of course. I always had known; I just didn't want to face it.

Mother had made her peace with life. And with death. Earlier, during the first days of her stay at the Terrace, antibiotics had been appropriate; Mother had unfinished work to do and she fought to live. She had spent years at the task of making a whole out of life. Now she had finished that work and she was fighting just as hard to be allowed to make a whole out of death.

But wasn't it too late?

There was a world of difference between the *passive* posture of never beginning a life-support procedure in the first place and the *active* move of withdrawing that support.

V
The Decision

V

Early the next morning I set out once again for Westminster Terrace. For some reason at the last moment I picked up my little travel Bible and put it in my briefcase. The same, brown-eyed nurse at the station on the second floor had a nametag on her uniform today, announcing that she was "Mrs. Brady." Mrs. Brady told me that Mother's condition had not changed.

Cennie was waiting. I stepped to Mother's bedside. She lay with her eyes closed, restlessly tugging at the mesh restraints.

"It's Johnny, Mother. Can you hear me?"

No response. A nurse came in and tested Mother's reactions.

"Mrs. Sherrill?"

No response. The nurse called more loudly. *"Mrs. Sherrill?"* She clapped her hands so smartly that I jumped. Still no response. The nurse made a note in her log and left the room.

I asked Cennie if she wouldn't like a cup of coffee and so began still another long set of hours with the unhearing, unheeding, thrashing, endlessly struggling figure in front of me. We "talked" for the first half hour, but again it was utter frustration.

In the end—once again—all I could do was hold her hand.

I found Cennie in Staff Dining and asked her to go back and sit with Mother. Then I headed toward the nurses' station in the center of the floor.

But why?

What could I hope to achieve?

All around me was the evidence of a well-run institution, the hollow loudspeaker sounds, the nose-smarting antiseptic smells, the shiny, well-scrubbed people and equipment. I was in the hands of an institution that was using "correct" procedure. I could no more reverse it than I could hope to turn the tide, and in any event I didn't know what I wanted to suggest.

Brown-eyed Mrs. Brady looked up. It was a pointless question but I asked it anyhow. "Isn't there anything we can *do*!" I said.

Mrs. Brady looked at her watch. "Perhaps you'd like to speak to Dr. Haller? He should be in his office."

As a matter of fact I *didn't* want to try bearding the lion, but I nodded and Mrs. Brady picked up the phone to place one of the pivotal telephone calls of my life. She explained to the Terrace's visiting physician that I'd gotten in from overseas, and that I'd seen Mother and needed to talk. She handed me the telephone and discreetly stepped to the far end of the station.

"Dr. Haller?"

The man's very first words were not at all lion-like. "I'm sorry about your mother," Dr. Haller said, "and I'm sure you have a lot of questions."

Encouraged, I started in. The diagnosis was pneumonia? Yes. And it was necessary to have Mother hooked up to those I.V.'s? The automatic medical response to pneumonia, Dr. Haller said, was to administer antibiotics, and in Mother's case, because of her prolonged resistance to taking the medication, this meant intravenously. I asked him if he knew of Mother's standing request not to resort to life-prolonging measures.

"No, we didn't get those instructions, and I'm afraid that's not unusual when you change institutions. Failures of communication. . . they do happen."

There was a long pause. And then, standing at the nurses' desk on the second floor of Westminster Terrace amid cheery signs of greeting ("Happy

Birthday, Mrs. Harris," "Happy Anniversary, Mr. Wills,") I asked the question I'd been avoiding.

"What would happen. . ." I tensed for an outraged reaction. "What would happen if we asked for those I.V.'s to come out?"

But there was no outrage. Dr. Haller's voice was neutral as he said, "The body does surprise us at times. But in my opinion, your mother would probably go ahead with her death."

My heart thumped, my head seemed tight. Dr. Haller did not hurry me. The Terrace's physical therapist stepped behind the desk and began to examine charts.

When Dr. Haller spoke again I realized how many, many times he and the staff at the Terrace must have been through this same agony. "There are some things you and your family will want to think about," he said.

Then Dr. Haller gave me three yardsticks.

The first was to consider Mother's own attitude. Had she come to terms with death? Was she reasonably at peace with herself and with others? The answer which I gave to myself was a resounding Yes.

"There's a second consideration," Dr. Haller said. "Suppose we do bring your mother back." I seized on this. Mother *had* come back once before. Couldn't it happen again? Dr. Haller went on. "The question we have to ask is, what would she come back *to*?"

I didn't answer, and Dr. Haller continued. "Would she come back to a rational, at least fairly satisfying life? Or would she come back to invalidism and some worse kind of deterioration? *That* can happen, too. When the body begins to go, we often pull it out of one crisis only to have it break down somewhere else, perhaps in a more painful, more dehumanizing way."

"She did recover from a supposedly irreversible condition four years ago."

"That can happen, and you have to allow for it."

"What do you think?" I asked, aware, even as I posed the question, that the previous diagnosis and the previous prognosis for Mother had both been wrong. "In your experience what *would* she come back to?"

"My opinion is that your mother's deterioration isn't going to stop."

I thought again about how important Mother's own attitudes were in this ongoing process. The body seemed to have a wisdom of its own, hearing different appropriate messages at different times. There was a startling contrast between Mother's attitude four years ago and now. Before, Mother had been fighting to return, to move downstairs, to get well. Now? Even though she couldn't speak, she clearly and precisely *acted* out her message.

"There is a third criterion," Dr. Haller's voice was saying. "If we took our the I.V.'s, how would *you* feel? How would you feel now. . . and later. You will have to live with whichever decision you make."

This was an aspect I had not considered before. I was to wish later that I'd paid more attention.

"Let me be sure again. . . " I said. This was impossible! "What exactly would happen if we did take out the I.V.'s?"

"The pneumonia would get worse. Let me tell you something about pneumonia, Mr. Sherrill. There's a saying among doctors that pneumonia is the old man's friend."

"What does that mean?"

"Nobody dies of 'old age.' We die of something specific. Pneumonia is a kind way to go. Relatively quick and painless. A friend when we need one most."

Suddenly the issues were not at all theoretical. If we removed the I.V.'s would we be taking on a responsibility that human beings should not assume? *Or was just the opposite true? In keeping elderly bodies alive artificially has mankind taken on a responsibility that should never have been ours?*

What did God want?

That, of course, was the central question. What was His intention! And how could we ever know?

Dr. Haller did not hurry me. Life went on, there at the nurses' station on the second floor at Westminster Terrace. A kitchen aide wheeled a cart of mostly-empty trays back to the elevator. The physical therapist snapped shut his chart. Mrs. Brady said, "Good morning," to a gentleman who came each day to see his wife.

"I'll make some calls," I said to Dr. Haller.

"All right. You'll let me know, then?"

"I will."

The words were heavy. Even as I spoke them the picture passed before my mind of that butterfly pinned, still struggling, to its specimen board.

I thanked Dr. Haller then handed the phone to Mrs. Brady. She spoke to the doctor for a moment, making notes in a log, then replaced the phone in its cradle.

I went back to Room 245. When I stepped through the door Cennie leaned down to Mother.

"John is here, Helen."

Mother gave no sign of understanding. Her fretful tugging at the restraints never ceased. Her hands were speckled with the brown spots Mother called, "age marks." The skin was no longer tight on her arms.

"I'm going to talk to the family, Mother, about getting out those I.V.'s," I said. "Do you understand what that means?"

No response.

"I'm going to call Mary and Tib and the children and Margaret." Margaret was Mary's mother-in-law, part of Mother's "Anchorage family." "But we believe we are hearing you clearly, Mother."

No response.

Downstairs there was a pay phone with a chair next to it. I pulled up the chair and began dialing. I called Mary and Hugh first. We talked at length, reviewing every phase of the conversation with Dr. Haller. Mary and I were in agreement. "I hated those I.V.'s from the first," she said. "They're all wrong for now." I then spoke to four of the six grandchildren—all I could reach—and to Mary's mother-in-law, Margaret Durham, and her daughter Lucia.

I didn't really put the question to a vote; that wouldn't have been fair. But I did outline the situation carefully, explaining what would happen if we withdrew the antibiotics. I reported that Mary and I both felt this was what Mother wanted, but begged anyone who saw the picture differently to speak out. Again and again, as I described Mother, members of the family would comment, "Not Grandmother!" "That's not right!" "She didn't want that!"

My last call was to Tib. I reached her on East Maui. She'd arrived from Hong Kong two hours earlier and was speechless at the news that Mother was tied to her bed. I couched the question of taking out the I.V.'s in such a way that she could easily object.

"It's her struggling that gets at me," Tib said. "She can't speak at all?"

"No."

"Not even with signs?"

"Nothing at all," I said.

"And how are you?"

"I'm just fine," I answered too quickly.

"Do you want me to come home? I can be there in a day."

But—although at the time I did not know why—I felt convinced that Tib should stay on in Hawaii. We'd gone through so much together: births, deaths, cancer, success, failure. Why was I so sure she should not be with me now? "Mother wouldn't even know you were here," I said.

I put the wall-phone receiver back into its shiny cup and sat still for a while. In all the calls there had not been a dissenting voice. At one time or another Mother had obviously made her wishes clear to each of us.

And so. . . no more stalling was possible.

I went back upstairs and told Mrs. Brady about our family decision. She put through a call to Dr. Haller, then handed me the phone.

"You reached your family?" said the doctor.

"Just about everyone. We all agree."

"Then I'll ask you please," the compassionate voice continued, "to get Mrs. Brady back on the phone."

I handed the instrument to Mrs. Brady who made some further notations in Mother's chart.

It was all so normal-seeming.

I walked down the polished floor to Room 245. Cennie looked up wearily. It was well past time for her to go home. "We're going to take the I.V.'s out," I told her.

The floor nurse, the same one who had tried to get a reaction from Mother before, came into the room. "Mrs. Sherrill?"

Mother did not even blink. Her wrists pulled at the strips of gauze.

I leaned down. "We're going to take those needles out now, Mother. The I.V.'s, the antibiotics." Her hands tugged ceaselessly.

The nurse took charge. "This may sting a little, Mrs. Sherrill. We'll take the tape off first, then the needles can come out. There. That wasn't bad. Now the other one."

The needles out, the nurse untied the first strip of gauze. I expected Mother's left arm to start flailing. So did the nurse apparently; she held Mother's free hand in her own, then released it. But this time Mother's hand did not move. Her whole left arm relaxed completely. The nurse looked at me. She went around the bed and unknotted the other strip of fabric. With that, Mother's whole being, starting with her hands and arms, virtually melted into total relaxation.

The nurse straightened up, staring. Cennie came to the bed, leaned over and kissed Mother on the cheek.

"Well, Mother. . ." I said.

Mother lay perfectly still, at peace. Her head no longer tossed, her hands lay palms down at her side.

When Cennie and the nurse had gone I spoke again. "It's done now, Mother. The I.V.'s are gone. But," I looked at the quiet hands, "I don't need to tell you that, do I?"

Mother was so very peaceful that I almost did not want to keep talking. Was it possible that she was this very moment making a transition to a new depth of being? Was she resting completely in the arms of her Lord?

I, however, was still very much part of the hustle and bustle of ordinary living, and before long I grew restless at just sitting still. But with Mother comatose there seemed little point in chatting.

Then I remembered that I'd brought my Bible with me from the motel. I could read to her!

So, I went over to Mother's half of the white dresser. Her world had shrunk to one mattress, one half of a dresser top and one yellow-and-gold Talisman rose in a white vase. I opened my briefcase and took out my travel Bible. I sat down again and unzipped it. What would Mother like to hear?

The Psalms, of course.

So, that April afternoon, I opened the Bible, very aware of our neighbor next door behind the curtain. I turned to the first Psalm and began to read, glancing up occasionally to look at Mother's tranquil face, her eyes closed, no longer in torment but in rest.

> Blessed is the man
> > who walks not in the counsel of
> > the wicked,
> nor stands in the way of sinners,
> > nor sits in the seat of scoffers;
> but his delight is in the law of the
> > Lord,
> and on his law he meditates day
> > and night.

Ps. 1:1-2

I looked up again. Mother's eyes were open!

Could I really be seeing this? They *were* open! I couldn't believe it. Her eyes were brilliant blue.

"Hello, Mother."

Her eyes looked deeply into mine, there in that all-white room. Her eyes didn't speak, they listened. It was like something I'd seen before. . . but what? The stare was steady. Unblinking.

"The I.V.'s are gone and your hands are free and I'm reading the Psalms to you, Mother. Can you understand what I'm saying?

The expression in her eyes did not change. They were not full of mental content but they were not vacant either. Mother's blue eyes, set deep into her face, held mine. What did they remind me of. . . ?

"Shall I go on?" Mother's eyes gave no message except to be open. More boldly now, oblivious of our roommate, I picked up the reading.

> *O Lord, how many are my foes!*
> *Many are rising against me;*
> > *many are saying of me,*
> *there is no help for him in*
> > *God.*
>
> *But Thou, O Lord, art a shield*
> > *about me,*
> *my glory, and the lifter of my*
> > *head.*

Ps. 3:1-3

Some passages were so incredibly apropos I could feel my voice thickening:

> *I lie down and sleep;*
> > *I wake again, for the Lord*

sustains me.
I am not afraid. . . .

Ps. 3:5,6

Thou has given me room when
  I was in distress.

Ps. 4:1

In peace I will both lie down and
    sleep;
for Thou alone, O Lord, makest
    me dwell in safety.

Ps. 4:8

There seemed to be a theme running through the Psalms I was reading, and the theme was God's protection. His oversight was not just of Mother but of me also. I couldn't get over the wonder of my sitting here by Mother's bedside when by rights I should have been on the other side of the world. At last it was clear not only why I had come home, but why that *particular* Thursday. Time was needed. I had to get over jet lag and adjusted to Stateside time zones. I needed to be emotionally and physically prepared for what was now taking place.

Mother's eyes remained open. They were living contentment. Twice, when nurses came in to take Mother's temperature and to turn her, I shifted my chair to the other side of the bed.

I read on into the afternoon, covering about a third of the Psalms. There continued to be places where the ancient hymns were so appropriate I couldn't believe they had not been written specifically for our situation.

> The cords of death encompassed
>   me,
> the snares of death confronted
>   me.
> In my distress I called upon the
>   Lord;
> to my God I cried for help.
> From his temple he heard my voice,
>   and my cry to him reached his ears.
>   Ps. 18:4-6 (portions)

By 5:00 that afternoon I was getting tired and so, I thought, was Mother. Although her azure eyes remained open they were heavy now.

So I zipped up my Bible, told Mother I'd see her in the morning, kissed her, and left. Her eyes followed, undisturbed, peaceful.

"How is she?" the duty nurse asked me from behind her desk and I answered that she was quiet. But as I was going down the stairs I knew that I hadn't been accurate. Mother was more than just quiet. I couldn't get her face out of my mind. What was there about those eyes. . . so penetrating, so steady, interested yet without challenge.

As I walked to the car I knew at last what it was. Mother's were the eyes of a *baby*.

I'd seen our children look at Tib and me that way

from their cribs when they were infants. There was the same intense alertness, the overwhelming awareness. You can't get in touch with a baby's mind, but you never doubt his awareness; and so it was with Mother. There is incredible wisdom in a baby's eyes; so there was in hers. There was age-lessness in Mother's look, just as in a newborn's. The baby is coming from God; Mother was going to God. And both conveyed to me the same whisper of eternity.

I arrived at the Terrace early, next morning, to find Cennie already there. We went out to the hall.

"Any change?"

"No. She slept well but she won't eat. Won't even swallow water."

"But she's quiet?"

"Very."

"She opened her eyes yesterday, Cennie! Looked at me for hours."

Cennie raised her brows. "She certainly hasn't opened them this morning."

I went into Mother's room and pulled my chair next to her bed. Cennie was right. Mother did not open her eyes, even when I told her the latest news about the children.

"I talked to Scott and Meg last night," I said. "Do you realize you have a grandson who is now a Columbia recording artist?" There was no response.

"Donn and Lorrie are starting an import business. Woolens and things from Peru!" Nothing. "Liz and Alan are fine. Liz will have her M.S.W. next May. Can you believe it? Still another generation getting into social work!"

Cennie came in. She took a hairbrush from her handbag, brushed Mother's hair, then stood at the foot of the bed. I unzipped my travel Bible. At the first words of the Psalm those blue eyes opened again.

"It's true," Cennie said softly. "It's true. It's almost like—like it was her own kind of food."

I started to read again. Cennie stayed on for a while, then stepped out.

For perhaps an hour Mother watched me with that baby's penetrating, alert, accepting gaze. I was reading more or less straight through the Psalms although I'd shorten some that were unusually long and reread others that were unusually germane. Yesterday I'd noticed the theme of protection running through the verses. Now, as I sat reading a new theme began to emerge. Repentance.

It was while I was reading Psalm 51 that a startling thing occurred. Unexpectedly, Mother's wide open, blue eyes filled with tears.

I was stunned, for here was the first direct communication. If not with me, then with God. I paused and reread the Psalm, my mind focused on what was being said:

> Have mercy on me, O God,
>   according to thy steadfast love;

according to thy abundant mercy
blot out my transgressions.
Wash me thoroughly from my iniquity,
and cleanse me from my sin!

Ps. 51:1,2

Dear Lord, what transgressions did this lady find weighing on her so heavily. Whatever they were they could not have been more devastating than David's, who wrote this plea at the point of his greatest sin:

For I know my transgressions
and my sin is ever before me.

Ps. 51:3

The tears continued flowing. How awed I was all over again at God's timing. If Mother had been fighting the life support systems she would never have had the internal leisure for the work she was now tackling. This was the "business of dying" people speak about. This was a happening, a gathering-in. I found myself praying that my own leave-taking would be as natural.

I knew, of course, that not every end could be so graceful; there is, after all, sudden death, pain-filled death. But I felt my conviction growing by the hour that if we had a chance for a natural death in the fullness of old age, we should not have the experience taken from us by wires and drugs and other well-meant intrusions. Dying should be as natural as birth, and I caught myself thanking God for this quiet coming-of-age in medicine that is restoring to death its rightness and dignity.

"Mother," I said, "you always did like to have your plans work out, didn't you!"

I stayed with Mother all day, then returned to my motel and phoned Tib in Hawaii. Her assignment was going well but slowly. I knew it was difficult for Tib not to be with Mother; they had a special one-to-one relationship. But her thoughts were not on herself. "It must be excruciating to sit there and watch your mother die," she said. "I feel I ought to be with you."

"You are with me. You know that."

"Yes, I do know it. In some strange way I've never felt so close to both of you."

Just how true this was we were not to know until later.

And now it was the last day; I was returning to New York tomorrow. Mary would be down next.

I thought I would feel distress at leaving Louisville, but it was all right. I had been called here from Hong Kong by a special kind of knowledge that by-passed the thinking mind. And now that same strange knowing allowed me to accept the fact that my assignment here was nearly over. There was a rounded-off-ness, a completion. Something had been accomplished.

What theme would emerge in the Psalms

today? What would follow the first themes of wonder at God's protection, and the deep-running liturgies of repentance?

I didn't start the reading immediately, that last day. During the morning I chatted now with Cennie, now with Mother, although Mother remained in a seeming coma, eyes closed, unstirring. The lunch tray came, but she would not open her mouth to take food. About one in the afternoon a nurse came in " . . . just to check on how you're doing, Mrs. Sherrill." Her voice was deliberately loud. No response. Later Cennie came in, her pocketbook over her arm. I wouldn't see her next morning since I had an early plane. Cennie fluffed Mother's pillow. I followed her into the polished hallway.

"I won't see you again for a while," I said.

"No," she said.

"Mary will be coming down later in the week."

"Yes."

She left.

"We love you, Cennie McClure," I whispered to her receding back.

I returned to Room 245 and sat down in the straight chair.

"Well, it's time for our last reading," I said moving the Bible's zipper along its track. I was no longer shy about our Bible time, but read in a normal voice:

> Make a joyful noise to the
> Lord, all the lands.

Serve the Lord with gladness.
Come into his presence with
singing.

Ps. 100: 1,2

I was afraid to look up, afraid to pursue the marvel of the wakeful eyes too far. She had not opened her eyes once today, no matter how much noise or how many people were in the room. Surely I was putting too much stock in this strange ironic gift of communication *through* the Bible when we'd always had so much trouble communicating *about* the Bible. But at last I did glance toward Mother.

Her eyes were looking straight at me. Wide open, unblinking, overwhelmingly aware.

"Oh God!" I said aloud, a prayer of two words.

That last afternoon Mother's eyes did not stay open for the entire, long reading time. By that very fact, though, she spoke to me about what was going on in her spirit. For today Mother's eyes opened only at the Psalms that spoke of praise and glory.

I came to the final five. Mother's eyes were open, blue and clear. Phrases stood out because they described events I was seeing before my very eyes:

The Lord sets the prisoners free;
the Lord opens the eyes of the
blind.
The Lord lifts up those who are
bowed down . . . .

Ps. 146:8

These last five Psalms were carillons. There
was a mounting crescendo to the words that peeled
before me:

> Praise the Lord!
> Praise the Lord from the
>   heavens.
> Praise him in the heights!
> Praise him, all his angels,
> praise him, all his host!
>
> Ps. 148: 1,2

I looked at Mother. I could almost imagine that
she was smiling as I began the very last hymn in the
book.

> Praise the Lord!
> Praise God in his sanctuary;
>   praise him in his mighty firma-
>   ment!
> Praise him for his mighty deeds . . . .
>
> Ps. 150: 1,2

I started to close the book but instead I took
Mother's hand in mine. I looked into those unblinking eyes, hoping that at this last moment Mother
might squeeze my hand. But that did not happen.
Her curled fingers remained at rest. Never mind.

I flipped back through the pages and read:

> The Lord is my shepherd, I
>   shall not want;

He makes me lie down in green
pastures.
He leads me beside still waters . . . .

Even though I walk through the
valley of the shadow of death,
I fear no evil;
for thou art with me . . . .

Surely goodness and mercy shall
follow me
all the days of my life;
and I shall dwell in the house
of the Lord
forever.

from Ps. 23

Now I closed the book. I kissed Mother on
the forehead and left the room.

VI
The Question

VI

I carried my bags up the slate steps. The house was stuffy and colder than the out of doors. I opened the windows to the April air, threw a frozen steak on the fire and began to unpack. All the while I kept reviewing the events of the past few days. I was certain that we had heard *Mother's* will in the matter—I was not quite so sure that we had heard *God's*.

I went downstairs to the empty kitchen and took the steak off too soon. It was cold in the center but I didn't bother to put it back on the fire.

Mother died peacefully three days after I returned home. The funeral was to be in Anchorage. It didn't make sense for Tib to travel 11,000 miles round trip for the funeral, but it was difficult to persuade her of this when I reached her in Hawaii. I reported a phone call with our son Donn. "Donn made a good point," I said over the phone. "I'll have a lot of support this week. If you came now, Donn pointed out, you'd have to go back to Hawaii later, just at the time I'd need you most. After everyone else is gone."

So Tib stayed in Hawaii.

The funeral was set for Tuesday, the day after tomorrow, and now I was walking through the waiting room at the airport in Louisville. Our daughter Liz's plane had come in just before mine and she'd made arrangements for a rental car. Our sons Donn and Scott were arriving tomorrow, Donn by plane from Rochester and Scott by bus from Nashville.

"How are you, Dad?" Liz asked as we drove through the dusk away from the rental lot. Liz wore her blonde hair in a new, bouncy, short style. "I mean, think about that a minute and then tell me how you really are."

So I thought before answering. Our route to Anchorage took us toward Cave Hill cemetery where my father had been buried nearly a quarter century ago, and where Mother would lie now, next to him. I was glad it was springtime. Dad called it nature's virginal hour. Mother would be buried in the midst of the blossoming jonquils and crabapple.

"To be really honest, Liz, the thought keeps bugging me that I've killed my mother."

Liz didn't jump all over me, dismissing the idea. "Because you let her die?"

"It's more active than that, Liz. We didn't just let her die. We asked the doctor to take out the I.V.'s."

"Yes," said Liz. "Because sometimes we have to undo what never should have been done in the first place." I didn't miss the fact that Liz said "we." She went on. "Doesn't it say somewhere in the Bible that there is 'a time to die'?"*

"Ecclesiastes," I said. I'd read that third chapter many times, this last week.

"That's a principle, then," said Liz. "It's not a decision we made by ourselves. We made it *with* God."

We were silent, speeding along the Waterson Expressway. I was remembering another verse in that same chapter of Ecclesiastes, a verse that seemed to shine with some hidden promise: "He has made everything beautiful in its time."**

Everything? Death too?

The physical details of death were often so unpleasant that it was hard to associate it with

---

*Ecclesiastes 3:2
**Ecclesiastes 3:11

beauty. Yet I remembered, even amid the antiseptic smells on Second, amid the wanderings of minds no longer sound and the sufferings of bodies no longer young, a bouquet of flowers at the nurses' station. . . the kindness of Cennie's touch. . . those uninterrupted hours when Mother and I shared the Psalms.

What if beauty were the signature of His season? Could some unexpected beauty tell us that we had, in fact, caught His timing?

Mary's mother-in-law, Margaret Durham, had offered us her Anchorage home as a base during this funeral week. I pulled the rented car into Margaret's driveway. The headlights picked out tulips in blossom. Inside, much of the family was already assembled. There were Margaret and her daughter and her other son from next door and his wife and their grown kids. Mary was there, (wearing her sensible Old Maine Trotters!) and her second son John with his wife and baby. Others were coming soon.

At first there was a sense of shyness, almost restraint, before the immense fact of death. Yes, we had eaten. Yes, Scott and Donn were coming in tomorrow. Mary's other son, Tom, and his wife were coming in tomorrow too. Yes, I was sure Margaret had done the right thing in reserving a room at the nearby Middletown Manor for me and the boys.

We talked about plans. We'd have to settle on

an order of service for the funeral.

"I know one hymn we must include!" said Mary.

At that moment the telephone rang. It was Mary's husband, Hugh, calling from Washington with his travel plans, and we never got back to the subject of the music.

The hymn came up again the next day. At noon Monday, after making arrangements with the funeral home, Mary and I drove back through the budding-maple lanes of Anchorage, past the century-old red brick Presbyterian church where the service would be held tomorrow, and pulled into Margaret's driveway. Cennie was there, red-eyed, and one other non-family guest, Dr. John Ames.

Dr. Ames had been pastor of the Anchorage Presbyterian Church for eight years. He was seated now, dressed in bluejeans and tennis shoes, on the edge of the sofa seat, a pad and pencil in his hand.

"John Ames had a special thing for your mother," whispered Margaret as she passed a plate of country ham sandwiches. "He came back from his vacation to be here. A hundred-mile drive, each way."

John Ames helped us through the logistical work of a death. Had we thought of the obituary? Flowers? Pallbearers? The order of service? We made decisions quickly.

"How about music?" John asked.

Two hymns were discussed and chosen.

"You said yesterday," I reminded Mary, "that one hymn was a special favorite?" Mary and Mother both played the piano and Mary was more in touch with Mother's musical preferences than I.

"Yes," Mary answered. "I remember her playing it over and over on the piano. . . ."

John Ames' pencil was poised.

"It was. . . ." To my amazement Mary looked as if she were about to cry. She stammered forth the name of the hymn so low I did not hear it.

John Ames spoke up. "Helen was one of the least sentimental people I've ever known," he said gently. "Her funeral ought to be a celebration! Let's not pick a song that makes everyone cry."

Mary blew her nose. "That's right," she said.

It did make sense; no one wanted to be maudlin, and it was true that John Ames' special relationship with Mother deserved to be listened to. Without further consideration, Mother's song was dropped from the order of service.

The funeral, Tuesday, was simple. The young men of the family acted as Mother's pallbearers. Cennie, of course, sat with the family. Four clergy friends of Mother's conducted the short service. John Ames spoke very briefly. Death, he said, is that unique point between time and timelessness when the Spirit of Christ can finally take total and permanent possession of us. The Apostle Paul, from prison, had written to one of his younger companions that he did not want to be an object of pity because death was at hand. "Don't feel sorry for me," he wrote, "that death is near. I have fought the good fight. I have finished the race."

Here, again, was the question of a natural termination. "The end—the *goal*," John was saying in summary, referring to St. Paul, but also to Mother, ". . . the purpose of life could not be achieved until death. And that goal? To be completely, fully, genuinely, 'in Christ.' "

John closed his notes. "We are grateful to God for life," he said, "and we are also grateful to God for death. For we know that however diminished *we* are, Helen has reached that natural end of her life which God ordained for her and for us as well."

Cave Hill cemetery was a burst of spring color. The grave site happened to be beneath two flowering fruit trees, one pink and one white, set against the kind of very-blue sky that seems to belong uniquely to Kentucky. We buried Mother there side by side with Dad.

VII
Mother's Song

VII

E ast Maui is the most beautiful place on earth. That's not just Tib's and my opinion; world traveler Charles Lindbergh chose a lonely stretch of this Hawaiian island for his retirement. He is buried in a tiny graveyard there.

The house where Tib was staying was an A-frame cabin on the volcanic slope above the Lindbergh's home. No road leads to it, only a jeep track through a cattle pasture. The cabin was built by Tay and Lowell Thomas, Jr. They had let us stay there a couple of years earlier, to work in a writer's version of paradise: no telephone, no radio or TV, enough

light from the kerosene lamp for one game of crib-
bage after supper, not enough to push bedtime past
nine o'clock.

The invitation to use the cabin again, just the
two of us, before Tay arrived to work on a book
project with Tib, had seemed like heaven opening a
second time. Which made it all the stranger that I
had so uncomplainingly obeyed that nudge which
had come to me in Hong Kong just before Mother's
death.

At any rate, Tib was at the cabin now, working
with Tay. And there on Maui the provision of every
need, which had been the hallmark of this whole
experience, continued to amaze us. Our needs, in
fact, were being met even before we knew they
existed.

Since our first visit to the cabin, for instance,
Tay's parents had stayed there. Neither of them in
good health, they had installed a telephone so that
now, with an almost daily need to reach Tib with
Mother's news, the means was there. It was Tay, in
fact, who answered the phone the day Mother died.

But if we were grateful for the telephone, an
even more mysterious provision was to follow. . . .

There was still no electricity in the cabin; Tib
and Tay regulated their days by kerosene-time. Tib
soon fell into a routine. Mornings she'd be at work
at 5:00. About 8:00 she'd brew a second pot of coffee
on the propane stove. Pouring it into a dented alu-

minum thermos, she'd set out into that breath-catching landscape to walk for a couple of hours before the joint work session began.

On this particular rainbow-filled morning, on the day of Mother's funeral, as she described it to me later, she followed the wheel-tracks down through the pasture and let herself out the cattle gate onto the rutted dirt road. There she turned left, past Lindbergh's grave, through a papaya grove. To her left rose extinct, cloud-shrouded Haleakala, its slopes streaked with thread-like waterfalls.

About two miles from where the cattle gate let onto the road she came to a swollen mountain torrent where she and I had often picnicked together. Here Tib left the road and followed a steep path up the side of the stream to a spot where the water cascades to a whirlpool far below. It is the tallest waterfall on the stream's journey and our favorite picnic spot. She sat down, legs dangling over the abyss, and uncorked the thermos.

Far below, to her right, stretched the endless Pacific, lavender in the morning light. But it was the waterfall to her left that riveted her attention. She watched the water burst from the screen of foliage and fling itself into space in a kind of slow-motion majesty, scattering into a thousand individual drops as it began its plunge.

She refilled the cup, then paused. Suddenly she was aware, she did not know how, that this was the very hour and moment of the funeral service. That she had made the coffee and come to sit beside these falls to be part of what was happening in Anchorage, Kentucky.

Her logic told her she could not possibly know this: I had told her the day of the funeral, but I had not mentioned whether the service was scheduled for morning, afternoon or evening. And yet with a certainty beyond logic she knew that the Durhams and I and our children were gathered at that moment in that red brick Presbyterian church. She looked at her watch—not so that she could check with me later; the certainty was too strong—but to picture in her mind the time of day it was in Kentucky. On Maui it was a few minutes past 9:00 A.M. Then in Kentucky it was two in the afternoon. . . .

Closing her eyes, she joined the family gathering. It was the first time she had admitted to herself how hard it was to be so far away. Only now did she let herself think about her own bereavement. We both believed that everything in God's time is beautiful. . . . so why, Tib wondered, couldn't it have worked out for her to be there?

The only answer was the thunder of the falls. Opening her eyes she gazed at the cascading water. The sun was high now; off to her right the sea glittered with diamonds.

And suddenly, the same way she knew the funeral was happening at that very moment, 5,000 miles away, she also knew something else. She knew, not with her mind but with her eyes and bones and heart, what Mother's experience had been like in those last speechless days at Westminster Terrace.

Because it was an experience rather than a thought, she had trouble putting it into words, for Tay later that day, and still later, for me. "The problem is, it sounds so trite when you talk about it. Like a cliché. But it didn't *feel* that way. It felt—unexpected, the way real things do."

What she experienced was Mother's life as though it were a drop of water in the stream before her. She reviewed the adventures of that droplet from its first inception in a raincloud. She followed it through a narrow rivulet high on the mountainside, saw the channel deepen as other drops joined the flow. Rapids, rocks, long straight stretches, swirling eddies, deep calm pools.

And now the ocean was in sight, the goal of it all: beckoning, sparkling, immeasurable. In front of where Tib sat with her feet dangling was the immense adventure of the waterfall, the joyful hastening of the waterdrop toward a very different kind of existence. The moment came to fling itself free of the stream, to launch itself in abandon into the air. Her eye followed a droplet as it caught the rising sun and flashed back the colors of the rainbow.

All was speeding up now, going rapidly, all was turbulence and agitation, until somewhere beyond where her eyes could follow, that drop of water encountered the all-embracing sea.

That would be a new experience for the journeying droplet. All at once the banks of the channel would no longer hem it in. The hurry it had felt through all its career to travel onward, to press ever forward, would be swallowed up in arrival. That would be the experience of eternity.

Tib shifted on the stream bank. She felt stiff, as though hours had passed. A lifetime. Yet, in the cup in her hand, the coffee was still hot.

She sipped it slowly, wondering. She had puzzled over why she could not be present at the formal farewell to someone she loved. Was this why? Had she been guided to this mountainside to sit beside a stream and share a last experience with Mother?

And still there was more to come, in this parable of physical separation, spiritual communion.

The morning after the experience at the waterfall, the coffee seemed to take forever to perk. Restlessly Tib scanned the bookshelf in the cabin's living-room-kitchen. Among the books was a blue-bound hymnal. "Music!" she thought, pulling it out and flipped through the pages. The one disadvantage to living without electricity was the lack of a phonograph.

It was not a hymn book she was familiar with, however. With over 600 songs to choose from, which one should she learn? Near the back of the book, her eye hit on the word *rainbow*. That sounded appropriate for Hawaii! In another verse was something about *sunshine*. And when she saw *ocean*, that settled it. Oceans and sunshine and rainbows! The very song for a morning walk on Maui.

Tib has an amazing memory for words (I know, having lost every argument over the exact phrase for 34 years). And so, as the coffee perked on the stove, she "photographed" the four verses of the unfamiliar hymn and worked out the melody. Then she filled the thermos and headed down the pasture.

At the road she again turned left, humming the tune over and over lest it escape her. (Melodies are harder for her to retain than lyrics.) At the stream she had visited yesterday, instead of climbing the hill to the waterfall, she turned right and followed the path downhill through pandanus trees with their stilt-like above-ground roots.

At the ocean's edge Tib sat on a black lava outcrop and poured her first cup of coffee. To her left she could see "Mother's stream" tumbling down out of the jungle. Just here, where the waves dashed themselves on the rocks, she let the song remind her of what she had known so clearly beside the waterfall.

Tib's singing voice, in her estimation, is so off-key, "I'm embarrassed even to have *me* hear me." But here was a situation made to order: the crash of the waves spared her ears the pain of her delivery. So, at the top of her lungs, she sang the first verse of the new hymn:

O Love that wilt not let me go,
    I rest my weary soul in Thee;
I give Thee back the life I owe,

That in Thine ocean depths its flow
May richer, fuller be.

It was the first time the words of the song had penetrated past her eyes and the mechanics of memorization. She sang the verse again, disbelievingly. Why—this song was for Mother! It was all about Mother; it was the very insight she had had beside the waterfall, the day before.

As she sang the second verse, tears mingled with the salt spray on her cheeks:

O Light that followest all my way,
    I yield my flickering torch to Thee;
My heart restores its borrowed ray,
    That in Thy sunshine's blaze its day
May brighter, fairer be.

How could she have stood there beside the stove, looking at these words and not *see* them! "Ocean" and "sunshine" indeed! The song was not about a Maui morning, but about returning—about reunion with the Source Himself.

Here in the third verse was the reference to "rainbow" that had first stopped the flipping pages of the hymnal:

O Joy that seekest me in pain,
    I cannot close my heart to Thee;
I trace the rainbow through the rain,
    And feel the promise is not vain
That morn shall tearless be.

Morn—why, it was morning now for Mother! A morning even more glorious than this gold and scarlet day at the edge of the sea. The final verse said it most clearly:

> O Cross that liftest up my head
>> I dare not ask to fly from Thee;
> I lay in dust life's glory dead,
>> And from the ground there blossoms
>> red
> Life that shall endless be.

Endless life—how exactly that fit the bright, endlessly alive person Tib knew! She sang the song all the way home along the rutted dirt road, all the way up the track through the cattle pasture. Tay was sitting on the deck watching a mongoose emerge from his hole. Tib brought out the hymnal from the kitchen counter and told Tay how she had memorized an entire song before she knew why.

"*O Love That Wilt Not Let Me Go*," Tay said, nodding. "It's one of my favorites."

"I'm surprised I never came across it before," said Tib. "Glad, too. For me it will always be Mother's song."

And Mother's song it was, the remaining ten days that she worked there in the A-frame on Maui. She sang it on her morning walks, and beneath the outdoor shower with the bougainvillea nodding overhead, and (silently) on her bed at night to the rhythm of the cattle cropping the grass. Whenever the ache of Mother's going struck her fresh, she let the song remind her of what she had known so clearly beside the waterfall.

I met Tib's plane at Kennedy Airport and all 50 miles of the drive home we talked like people who'd been separated three years instead of three weeks. I wanted to hear everything she'd done since I said goodbye to her in Hong Kong; she wanted every detail of my last visit with Mother. We'd covered the facts over the phone, but now the way we felt about the facts came tumbling out.

"I had such a feeling," I said, "of watching a process that had already begun, way before the point where I came in."

"What time of day was the funeral?" Tib asked suddenly.

"What time? Two in the afternoon."

"Yes. . . ." And then she told me about sitting by the waterfall while I was in the church in Anchorage, and following a drop of water with her eyes. "It was just what you said! A process—going faster, starting to race, leaping—oh honey, the waterfall was the climax! To dam the water there . . force it back. . . then the song wouldn't fit or anything!"

"Song?" I asked.

"Mother's song." She cleared her throat. "If you promise not to laugh at my voice I'll sing it for you."

Of course I didn't laugh. Soon I was humming the tune along with her. And fighting down a far-fetched idea that kept popping into my mind. Could this possibly be the beauty I'd been looking for, the beauty that was the token that we had indeed found His timing?

We were still singing as I swung the car down our steep driveway and began hauling suitcases from the trunk.

"And you say you've been singing it all week?"

"More than a week."

The idea would not stay down. In the house I picked up the telephone and dialed my sister in Washington.

"Mary? Just wanted to report Tib home safe and sound. And... Mary, do you remember that hymn you wanted in the funeral service? The one that was taken out? What was the name of it?

"The one Mother liked so much?"

"That's right."

"*O Love That Wilt Not Let Me Go*." said Mary. "And you know," she went on, "I've felt bad about it. Everything else was so right. But I'm sorry that hymn was left out."

"It wasn't left out, Mary," I assured her. "Nothing was left out at all."

THE
END

And now, there's something else I'd like you to read

VIII

Six Points to Think About

VIII

I have put *Mother's Song* down on paper not because our story is extraordinary or dramatic but for just the opposite reason. This is our individual experience, but at the same time the story is typical, almost universal. All of us are in this story somewhere. All of us face death and the death of loved-ones and the fear-filled or hope-filled question of what the very end of life will be like.

These issues have been with mankind forever. Today however, they are edged with a new tension. For today *we* play a part in determining the timing of death. For the first time in history we must look at the question of when life-prolonging measures should be used, and when not.

We came to the end of this experience feeling that if we didn't have answers, at least we'd isolated some of the right questions. We have committed ourselves to consider them now, today, while we are healthy and alert.

1. If doctors are able to help an elderly person through a health crisis, what does he return *to*? Will it be to a life of reason and tolerable health, or will it be to new breakdown and deterioration and pain?

   This is a medical opinion, and (as happened to Mother in 1977) this prognosis can be wrong. It does occur from time to time that a supposedly irreversible condition will turn around.

2. What does the person himself want? Has he expressed a desire to live just as long as possible, no matter what the means? Or does he want to be allowed to die *without* using the extraordinary aids that are available to us today?

   How do we *know* what a person wants? In our family we have made up our minds that we are going to share with each other our feelings about dying.

Living Wills are another way.* A Living Will is intended for a specific purpose. It is designed to expess a person's feelings about the use of heroic measures in the event that he cannot speak for himself.

3. What is the person's attitude *now*?

Our feelings may change as death approaches. Even if we are unable to speak there are innumerable ways to communicate, as we discovered with Mother. She expressed her readiness to be "gathered to her people," (to use the Bible's phrase,) in nonverbal ways: refusing food, rejecting medication.

4. What is the attitude of the family?

In our case, Mother had done her work well. No relationship is one hundred percent free of guilt and ambivalence. Have these been worked through to a reasonable degree? Mother knew that there were relationships that needed mending. When her time to die did arrive, she had completed most of that work.

---

*For a free copy of a Living Will, somewhat more complete than Mother's, send a stamped, self-addressed envelope to Chosen Books, Lincoln, Virginia, 22078.

5. What is God's timing?

We found that His signature is beauty, even in the midst of pain and sorrow. In Mother's passing we encountered example after example ("coincidences," kindnesses, unusual provisions). They were His encouragements, we believe now, that we had correctly interpreted the signs of His time.

6. Is death the end?

This is the question, of course, that affects all the others. Facing death is entirely different for someone who believes that there is an afterlife.

Since this is a personal story, I want to say that I have answered this question for myself with resounding conviction.

Death is not the end. Life continues on, richer and fuller. I will see Mother again. I will see Dad. And my Tib and our children, too. Once I came to this conclusion I found that although I still needed to face a great many questions about the *process of dying*, death itself receded in my thinking.

Having answered yes to life, the fear of death has simply vanished.

John Sherill

MY FRIEND, THE BIBLE

Although John and Elizabeth Sherrill were highly respected as creative Christian writers, John had problems. 'In spite of the fact that I had been a Christian for years,' he admits, 'I still did not feel really comfortable with Scripture.'

Then, urgently seeking personal help, he found that certain verses were highlighted as he read, 'as if the Bible were mysteriously activated, so that a portion was charged with power.'

Here he recounts how the Bible has sustained him: with Manna Verses, for a specific occasion, and Arsenal Verses, to be stored in the memory.

'Should send Christians to their Bibles with eyes wide open and ears unblocked.'

Church of England Newspaper

Charles Blair
(with John and Elizabeth Sherrill)

THE MAN WHO COULD DO NO WRONG

Here told for the first time is the story of an empire's collapse. It was a religious empire and the road to disaster was paved with the kind of intentions every reader will recognise. 'When I faced obstacles I tried to "believe",' explains Charles Blair. 'I made the mistake of having faith in faith. What I needed was faith in God.' Faith in faith led Charles to a courtroom, his church over-extended financially, with no money left to complete the Christian hospital he had been so convinced that God wanted built. From the nightmare of bitter public humiliation, Charles finally comes through to a glorious rediscovery of the love of God.

'Charles came to stand in our minds for every one of us caught in the trap of his own image. Needing to appear successful, wise, happy – allowing ourselves no room for failure. His story could be all our stories, but written in block capitals: few of us have started with so little, achieved so much, lost so publicly ...' *John and Elizabeth Sherrill.*

Brother Andrew

GOD'S SMUGGLER

'A book you will not want to miss.' *Catherine Marshall*

A story of exuberant, danger-charged adventure for Christ, which has become a bestseller.

Brother Andrew grew up in a devoutly Christian home in a tiny town in Holland. He is now 'God's Smuggler', carrying contraband Bibles past armed border guards into Communist countries. His own account of his mission to bring the love of Christ to the people behind the Iron Curtain makes compelling reading.

Corrie Ten Boom
(with John & Elizabeth Sherrill)

THE HIDING PLACE

The inspirational bestseller about the 50 year-old heroine of the anti-Nazi underground.

As the Nazi madness swept across Europe, a gentle family of watchmakers, the ten Booms, saw the lights go out of a free Holland. Read how the family were a channel of God's love in a world torn by fear, how they concealed the persecuted Jews in a special 'hiding place' and paid the price when their activities were discovered by the Nazis. Corrie's story will move every reader, as she tells how God's strength upheld her and her sister Betsie even in Ravensbrück.

E. M. Blaiklock

BETWEEN THE SUNSET AND THE STARS

Some prefer not to think about old age, and fear or despise it. Others, no longer young, despair of their failing limbs and bitterly regret the loss of youth. E. M. Blaiklock, 'between the sunset and the stars', sees his own ageing in the context of life's varied richness, as given by God. He affirms that old age can be as vital and fruitful as any other part of life.

'Old age is a psychological as well as a biological condition, and it can be successfully resisted by the brave. Rooted in biblical teaching, illuminated by wide classical and literary knowledge, *Between the Sunset and the Stars* is a book to reassure and encourage.

R. T. Kendall

TITHING

R. T. Kendall believes that all Christians are called to tithe. What is more, if all Christians did begin to tithe, he is convinced that the church would be revitalised and the world transformed. Dr Kendall combines this bold claim with the biblical, theological and practical implications of tithing.

'It is surprising how little has been written on this subject,' he writes. 'Most Christians have heard about tithing but how many have looked at it carefully?'

Tithing is sometimes regarded as threatening, but it emerges in this book as both challenging and inspiring. Numerous exciting testimonies are told, all demonstrating in individual lives the principle which underlies *Tithing*: 'You cannot out-give the Lord'.

Richard More

GROWING IN FAITH

The Lee Abbey Story.

As the Second World War was coming to an end, a group of Christians made a commitment to purchase a run-down hotel on the coast of North Devon. They had no money, and many of their friends felt that their plans were doomed to fail. Thirty-six years later the name of Lee Abbey is known all over the world as a centre for evangelism and as an agent for renewal in the church.

This book, tracing the development of the ministry of Lee Abbey, is a story of daring faith in God. The first account of Lee Abbey to be published for 25 years, it records the way God has brought new life into the church during five turbulent decades.

RICHARD MORE has for the last four years been a Chaplain at Lee Abbey.

Donald Bridge and David Phypers

MORE THAN TONGUES CAN TELL

The sequel to Spiritual Gifts and The Church. *Foreword by David Watson*.

Pastor and Deacon of Enon Baptist Church in Sunderland, Donald Bridge and David Phypers were 'deeply hesitant about Pentecostalism'. They were cautious, faced with the first charismatic prayer group in the church. But gradually, after serious Bible study and careful prayer a new dimension of Christian living transformed their lives and the life of the fellowship.

First encounters with supernatural activities are complemented by clear reflection and thorough biblical teaching. Years of prejudice are broken down as they learn to love Catholic charismatics. Finally the renewal movement is assessed, and pointers to future growth identified.